FOR CHILDREN'S WORKERS, PARENTS AND TEACHERS

The Big Book of Bible Crafts

INCLUDES PROJECTS FOR CHILDREN FROM PRESCHOOL TO SIXTH GRADE

COLORFUL PROJECTS WITH BIBLE STORY THEMES

COMPILED BY KIM SULLIVAN FIANO

Gospel Light

ACRYLIC PAINT

HOW TO MAKE
CLEAN COPIES FROM THIS BOOK

YOU MAY MAKE COPIES OF PORTIONS OF THIS BOOK WITH A CLEAN CONSCIENCE IF

- you (or someone in your organization) are the original purchaser;
- you are using the copies you make for a non-commercial purpose (such as teaching or promoting your ministry) within your church or organization;
- you follow the instructions provided in this book.

HOWEVER, IT IS ILLEGAL FOR YOU TO MAKE COPIES IF

- you are using the material to promote, advertise or sell a product or service other than for ministry fund-raising;
- you are using the material in or on a product for sale; or
- you or your organization are not the original purchaser of this book.

By following these guidelines you help us keep our products affordable.
Thank you,
Gospel Light

☼ Gospel Light

Publisher, William T. Greig
Senior Consulting Publisher, Dr. Elmer L. Towns
Publisher, Research, Planning and Development, Billie Baptiste
Managing Editor, Christy Weir
Senior Consulting Editors, Dr. Gary S. Greig, Wesley Haystead, M.S.Ed.
Senior Editor, Theological and Biblical Issues, Bayard Taylor, M.Div.
Editor, Kim Sullivan Fiano
Associate Editor, Karen Stimer
Assistant Editor, Linda Bossoletti
Designer, Lori Hamilton

CONTENTS

SECTION ONE/PREKINDERGARTEN-KINDERGARTEN
CRAFTS FOR YOUNG CHILDREN

CONTENTS

INTRODUCTION TO
THE BIG BOOK OF BIBLE CRAFTS

BIBLE CRAFT CREATIONS

Children love to make things; and as a parent, teacher or craft leader, one of the most important gifts you can give your children is to encourage their artistic expression. *The Big Book of Bible Crafts* will give your children the opportunity for creativity while reinforcing Bible truths, stories and Bible verses. Children and adults alike learn while *doing*. Although cutting, gluing and coloring may seem like child's play, your children will learn and retain their Bible lessons through these hands-on activities.

The *Big Book of Bible Crafts* is divided into two sections—Crafts for Young Children (Prekindergarten-Kindergarten children) and Crafts for Elementary Children (Grades 1-6). In each section, these Bible-related crafts are arranged in biblical order. We hope that you and your students will enjoy many fun-filled hours creating these projects from *The Big Book of Bible Crafts*.

PERSONALIZE IT!

We encourage you to use *The Big Book of Bible Crafts* as a basis for your craft program. You, as the teacher, parent or craft leader, play an essential role in leading enjoyable and successful craft projects for your children.

Feel free to alter the craft materials and instructions to suit your children's needs. Consider what materials you have on hand, what materials are available in your area and what materials you can afford to purchase. In some cases, you may be able to substitute materials you already have for the suggested craft supplies.

In addition, don't feel confined to the crafts in a particular age-level section. You may want to adapt a craft for younger or older age levels by utilizing the simplification or enrichment ideas provided for certain crafts.

THREE STEPS TO SUCCESS

What can you do to make sure craft time is successful and fun for your children? First, encourage creativity in each child! Remember, the process of creating is more important than the final product. Provide a variety of materials with which children may work. Allow children to make choices on their own. Don't expect every child's project to turn out the same. Don't insist that children "stay in the lines."

Second, choose projects that are appropriate for the skill level of your students. Children become easily discouraged when a project is too difficult for them. Keep your children's skill levels in mind when choosing craft projects. Finding the right projects for your students will increase the likelihood that all will be successful and satisfied with their finished products.

Finally, show an interest in the unique way each child approaches a project. Affirm the choices he or she has made. Treat each child's final product as "very creative"!

The comments you give a child today can affect the way he or she views art in the future—so make it positive! Remember: The ability to create is part of being made in the image of God, the ultimate creator!

BIBLE BITS

Each craft in this book includes a section entitled *Bible Bits*. These sections are designed to help you enhance craft times with thought-provoking conversation that is age appropriate. The conversation relates to the Bible story that each craft represents and will reinforce your children's Bible learning. If your craft program includes large groups of children, you may want to share these conversation suggestions with each helper who can in turn use them with individuals or small groups.

CRAFTS WITH A MESSAGE

Many of the projects in *The Big Book of Bible Crafts* can easily become crafts with a message. Children can create slogans or poetry as part of their projects; or you may want to provide photocopies of an appropriate poem, thought or Bible verse for children to attach to their crafts. Below are some examples of ways to use verses and words to enhance the craft projects in this book.

BE PREPARED

IF YOU ARE PLANNING TO USE CRAFTS WITH A CHILD AT HOME, HERE ARE THREE HELPFUL TIPS:

- Focus on the crafts in the book designated for your child's age, but don't ignore projects that are listed for older or younger ages. Elementary-age children enjoy many of the projects geared for preschool and kindergarten children. And younger children are always interested in doing "big kid" things. Just plan on working along with the child, helping with tasks the child can't handle alone.

- Start with projects that call for materials you have around the house. Make a list of the items you do not have that are needed for projects you think your child will enjoy. Plan to gather those supplies in one expedition.

- If certain materials seem too difficult to obtain, a little thought can usually lead to appropriate substitutions. Often the homemade version ends up being an improvement over the original plan.

IF YOU ARE PLANNING TO LEAD A GROUP OF CHILDREN IN DOING CRAFT PROJECTS, KEEP THESE HINTS IN MIND:

- Choose projects that will allow children to work with a variety of materials.

- Make your selection of all projects far enough in advance to allow time to gather all needed supplies in one coordinated effort. Many projects use some of the same items.

- Make up a sample of each project to be sure the directions are fully understood and potential problems can be avoided. **You may want to adapt some projects by simplifying procedures or varying the materials required.**

- Many items can be acquired as donations from people or businesses if you plan ahead and make your needs known. Many churches distribute lists of needed materials to their congregations and communities and are able to provide craft supplies at little or no cost. Some items can be brought by the children themselves.

- In making your supplies list, distinguish between items that each individual child will need and those that will be shared among a group.

- Keep in mind that some materials may be shared among more than one age level, but this works only if there is good coordination between the groups. It is extremely frustrating to a teacher to expect to have scissors, only to discover another group is using them. Basic supplies that are used repeatedly in craft projects, such as glue, scissors, felt pens, etc., should usually be provided to every group.

HELPFUL HINTS

USING GLUE WITH YOUNG CHILDREN

Since preschoolers have difficulty using glue bottles effectively, you may want to try one of the following procedures. Purchase glue in large containers (up to one-gallon size).

a. Pour small amounts of glue into several shallow containers (such as margarine tubs or the bottoms of soda bottles).

b. Dilute glue by mixing a little water into each container.

c. Have children use paintbrushes to spread glue on their projects.

glue level   swabs

OR

a. Pour a small amount of glue into a plastic margarine tub.

b. Give each child a cotton swab. The child dips the cotton swab into the glue and rubs glue on project.

c. Excess glue can be poured back into the large container at the end of each session.

CUTTING WITH SCISSORS

When cutting with scissors is required for crafts, take note of the fact that some of the children in your class may be left-handed. It is very difficult for a left-handed person to cut with scissors that were designed to be used with the right hand. Have available in your classroom two or three pairs of left-handed scissors. These can be obtained from a school supply center.

USING ACRYLIC PAINTS

Acrylic paints are required for several of the projects. Our suggestions:

• Provide smocks or old shirts for your children to wear, as acrylics may stain clothes.

• Acrylics can be expensive for a large group of children. To make paint go further, squeeze a small amount into a shallow container and add water until mixture has a creamy consistency. Or you may use acrylic house paints.

• Fill shallow containers with soapy water. Clean paintbrushes before switching colors and immediately after finishing project.

Craft projects for young children are a blend of "I wanna do it myself!" and "I need help!" Each project, because it is intended to come out looking like a recognizable something, usually requires a certain amount of adult assistance—in preparing a pattern, in doing some cutting, in preselecting magazine pictures, in tying a knot, etc. The younger the child, the more the adult will need to do, but care must always be taken not to rob the child of the satisfaction of his or her own unique efforts. Neither must the adult's desire to have a nice finished project override the child's pleasure at experimenting with color and texture. Avoid the temptation to do the project for the child or to improve on the child's efforts.

Some of the crafts have enrichment and simplification ideas included with them. An enrichment idea provides a way to make the craft more challenging for the older child. A simplification idea helps the younger child complete the craft more successfully. If you find a child frustrated with some of the limitations of working on a structured craft—although most of the projects in this book allow plenty of leeway for children to be creative—a child's frustration may be a signal that the child needs an opportunity to work with more basic, less structured materials: blank paper and paints, play dough or abstract collages (gluing miscellaneous shapes or objects onto surfaces such as paper, cardboard or anything else to which glue will adhere). Remember the cardinal rule of thumb in any task a young child undertakes: *The process the child goes through is more important than the finished product.*

"THINGS GOD MADE" BOOK
(15-20 MINUTES)

Materials
- Fun Foam in various colors
- wide-tip permanent felt pens

For each child—
- five resealable plastic sandwich bags
- several flat nature items (leaves, flowers, small pebbles, etc.)

Standard Supplies
- craft glue
- scissors
- stapler and staples
- ruler

Preparation: Cut Fun Foam into 7×12-inch (17.5×30-cm) rectangles—one for each child. Cut colored Fun Foam into a variety of small triangles and squares, about 1 inch (2.5 cm) in size. Lay five sandwich bags directly on top of one another with openings facing same direction. Staple bags together at sides opposite of openings (sketch a).

Instruct each child in the following procedures:
- Fold each Fun Foam piece in half to make book cover. Use felt pen to letter "Things God Made" on front of cover (sketch b).
- Lay bags inside the folded cover with the stapled edges along the fold. Staple all layers together along fold (sketch b).
- Glue foam shapes around the edge of book to make a border (sketch c).
- Place nature items in bags.

Enrichment Idea: Take children on a nature walk to collect items for their books.

Bible Bits: **What is one of your favorite things that God made, (Jessica)? We can learn about God by looking at the wonderful things He makes. We can also learn about God by listening to the stories in the Bible.**

a.

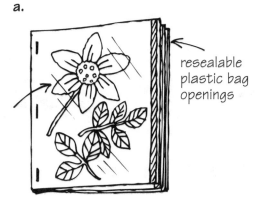

nature objects inside bags

resealable plastic bag openings

b.

Fun Foam

staples

c.

"GARDEN OF EDEN" PICTURE
(20-25 MINUTES)

Materials
- large sheets of black construction paper
- chalk in various colors including brown, green and blue
- aerosol hair spray
- animal crackers
- green netting
- blue foil wrapping paper
- small twigs
- cotton balls
- sand
- several plastic spoons

Standard Supplies
- glue
- scissors
- shallow containers

Preparation: Cut netting and foil paper into a variety of small shapes and place on table. Pour sand into shallow containers. Place a spoon in each container of sand. Place animal crackers, cotton balls and twigs in separate containers.

Instruct each child in the following procedures:
- Use chalk to color the background for garden picture on black construction paper. Color sky blue. Color dirt brown. Color grass green.
- When completed, teacher sprays picture with hair spray in well-ventilated area to set chalk. Let dry.
- Glue on twigs for tree trunks and green netting for foliage. Glue on pieces of blue foil paper for water and cotton balls for clouds.
- Squeeze glue on brown chalk areas and sprinkle sand over glue. With teacher's help, pour excess sand back into container.
- Glue animal crackers on picture.

Bible Bits: What animals did you put in your Garden of Eden Picture, (Marta)? God made all the animals. What other things did God create?

green netting

cotton balls

foil paper

animal crackers

The Big Book of Bible Crafts

LONG-NECK GIRAFFE

(15-20 MINUTES)

Materials
- Giraffe Pattern
- brown yarn

For each child—
- two wooden clothespins (spring-type)

Standard Supplies
- photocopier
- yellow card stock
- brown crayons or felt pens
- glue
- scissors
- ruler

Preparation: Photocopy Giraffe Pattern onto card stock—one for each child. Cut yarn into 2-inch (5-cm) lengths—one for each child.

Instruct each child in the following procedures:
- Cut out giraffe.
- Color brown spots on giraffe's body and neck.
- Glue yarn in place for tail.
- With teacher's help, fold giraffe's neck accordion style as in sketch.
- Clip clothespins onto bottom of giraffe's body to make legs.

Simplification Idea: Teacher cuts out the giraffes for younger children.

Bible Bits: **God created giraffes to have long necks. Why do you think God made their necks so long?** (To eat the leaves at the top of tall trees.) **What animals did God make that have long noses? long tails? lots of fur?**

clothespins

GIRAFFE PATTERN

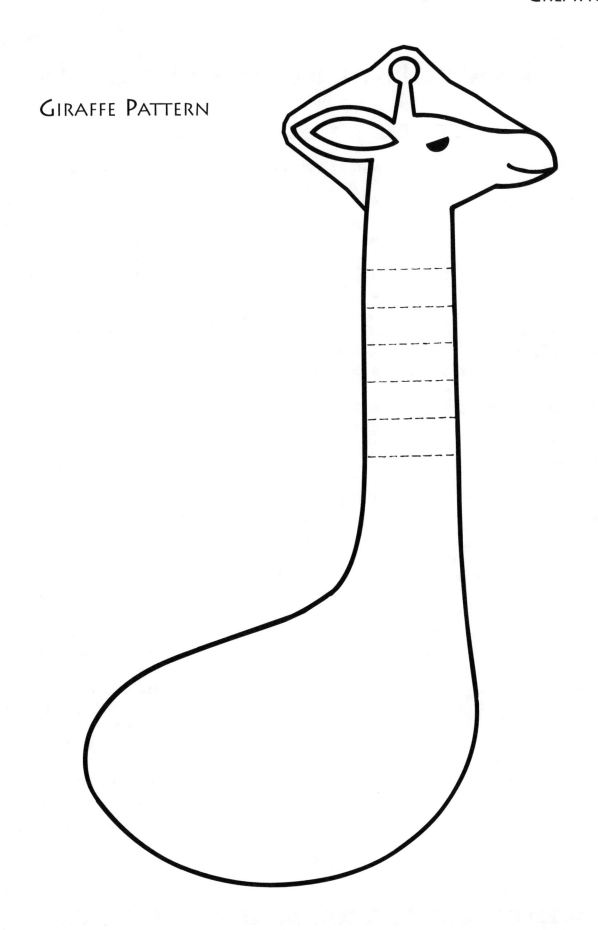

CRAWLING CREATURES BUG JAR
(15-20 MINUTES)

Materials
- Circle Pattern
- window screen
- colored tissue paper
- black and green permanent felt pens
- hammer and nail or drill and drill bit
- chenille wire

For each child—
- one plastic peanut butter or instant coffee jar with a 2¾-inch (6.9-cm) -wide mouth
- standard-size mason jar band

Standard Supplies
- craft glue
- scissors
- ruler
- damp paper towels

Preparation: With felt pen, trace Circle Pattern onto screen and cut out—one for each child. Use hammer and nail or drill to make two small holes opposite each other near the top of each jar (sketch a). Cut colored tissue paper into 2×4-inch (5×10-cm) rectangles— approximately eight for each child.

Instruct each child in the following procedures:
- Glue screen to the inside of the mason jar band. Let dry.
- Use green felt pen to draw grass around the bottom of the jar (sketch b).
- Crumple tissue pieces to form flowers.
- Glue flowers to the grass on jar (sketch b).
- Use a damp towel to clean excess glue off jar.
- With teacher's help, poke ends of chenille wire through the holes in the jar. Bend the ends of the chenille wire inside of jar to keep it from slipping out.
- Using a black permanent felt pen, teacher letters "Bugs" on the side of the jar (sketch c).
- Collect bugs to keep in jar. Be sure to provide your bugs with leaves and water.
- Screw on the bug jar lid.

Enrichment Ideas: Older children may enjoy using tissue paper and twist ties to make butterflies, snails and spiders (see sketches).

To make butterfly: Place a twist tie around the middle of a piece of tissue paper. Twist the tie together several times. Curl the tips of the tie to make antennae.

To make spider: Cut two twist ties in half. Twist the four pieces together in the middle and bend to make legs. Crumple a piece of tissue for body. Glue body to legs.

To make snail: Twist piece of tissue paper into a rope. Coil the rope to make a snail shell. Fold twist tie in half and place around bottom of coiled tissue. Twist ends of twist tie to make antennae. Glue butterflies, snails and spiders to jar or place inside jar.

Bible Bits: **God made every living creature. He made birds that fly, fish that swim and bugs that crawl. What kinds of bugs do you like, (Andrew)? You can collect some bugs and put them in your jar. After you watch them for a while, you can let them go outside and then catch some more bugs! God made lots of different insects for us to enjoy.**

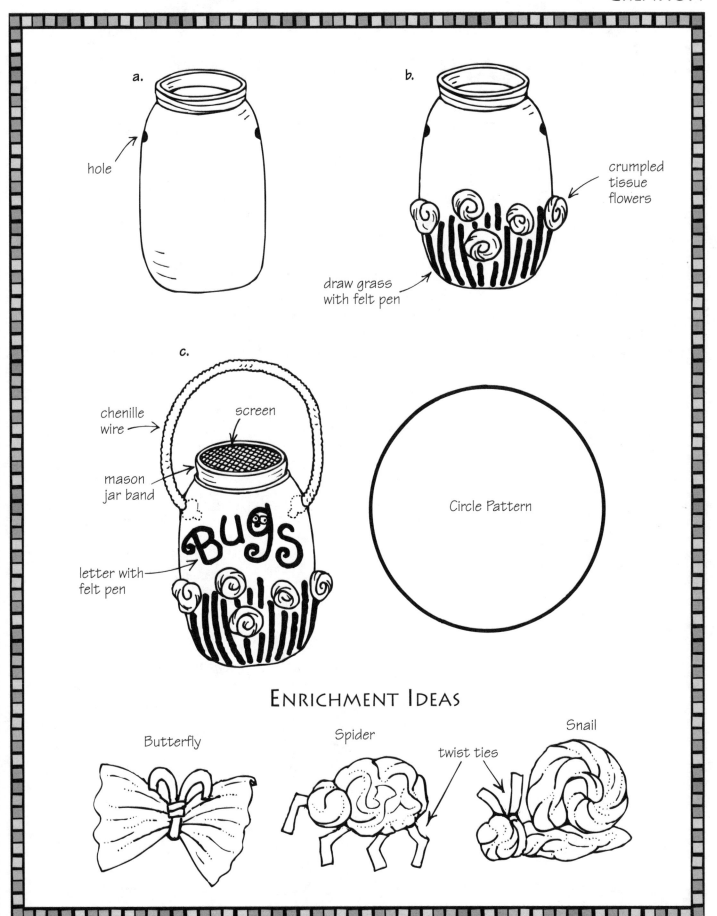

a.

hole

b.

crumpled
tissue
flowers

draw grass
with felt pen

c.

chenille
wire

screen

mason
jar band

Circle Pattern

letter with
felt pen

BUGS

ENRICHMENT IDEAS

Butterfly

Spider

Snail

twist ties

HANDPRINT BANNER
(15-20 MINUTES)

Materials
- felt in various colors including white
- sewing machine and thread
- yarn
- tempera paint
- squeeze bottles of fabric paint
- straight pins
- plastic-coated paper plates

For each child—
- one drinking straw

Standard Supplies
- scissors
- measuring stick
- water and soap for cleanup
- paper towels
- newspaper

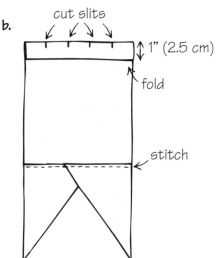

a. cut in half
4½" (11.25 cm)
6" (15 cm)

b.
cut slits
1" (2.5 cm)
fold
stitch

Preparation: Cut white felt into 7×9-inch (17.5×22.5-cm) rectangles—one for each child. Cut colored felt into 4½×6-inch (11.25×15-cm) rectangles—one for each child. Cut each colored rectangle into two triangles by cutting in half diagonally (sketch a). Lay short sides of triangles over bottom edge of white banner rectangle, overlapping in the center and making outer edges of triangle even with banner. Pin in place. Machine stitch triangles to banner (sketch b). Fold over 1 inch (2.5 cm) at the top of banner. Cut four equally spaced ⅛-inch (.3125-cm) slits in fold (sketch b). Cut yarn into one 28-inch (70-cm) length and four 12-inch (30-cm) lengths for each child. Cover work area with newspaper. Pour paint onto paper plates.

c.
drinking straw
Herbie

Instruct each child in the following procedures:
- Weave the straw through slits in the banner (sketch c).
- With teacher's help, tie one end of the long length of yarn onto each of the straw ends.
- Tie two short lengths of yarn onto each end of straw for tassels.
- Dip hand into the paint on paper plate. Print your hand in the center of felt banner.
- Wash and dry hands.
- Teacher letters child's name on banner with fabric paint. Allow to dry overnight.

Simplification Idea: Instead of sewing, use hot glue or craft glue to assemble banner.

Enrichment Idea: Children decorate triangle flags with fabric paint or glue on small felt shapes, acrylic jewels or sequins.

Bible Bits: **(Julia), your banner is different from everyone else's because it has your own handprint on it. God made everyone special. (Emily) has (brown) hair. Who has hair that is a different color? Whose hair is the same color?**

RAINBOW GLASS VASE
(20-25 MINUTES)

Materials
- craft tissue paper in various colors
- liquid starch
- clear acrylic spray

For each child—
- one small glass soda or sparkling water bottle

Standard Supplies
- sponge brushes
- scissors
- ruler
- shallow containers
- newspaper

Preparation: Cut tissue paper into 1½-inch (3.75-cm) squares. Cover work area with newspaper. Pour liquid starch into shallow containers.

Instruct each child in the following procedures:
- Paint the outside of glass bottle with starch.
- Place a tissue paper square over starch at neck of bottle.
- Gently paint more starch on top of tissue and smooth out any wrinkles.
- Working from top to bottom of bottle, continue applying paper squares to starch and smoothing out wrinkles as needed. Let dry.
- In a well-ventilated area, teacher sprays vases with clear acrylic spray.

Bible Bits: **Your Rainbow Glass Vase has many pretty colors on it, just like a rainbow! God put a rainbow in the sky as a promise to Noah that He would never send another flood to cover the earth. Every time you see a rainbow you can remember God's promise and that He loves you, too!**

NOAH'S RAIN CLOUD
(25-30 MINUTES)

Materials
- Sun Pattern
- crepe-paper streamers in six rainbow colors
- yarn

Standard Supplies
- blue crayons
- yellow construction paper
- white butcher paper
- pencil
- white glue or glue sticks
- scissors
- hole punch
- measuring stick
- paper towels

Preparation: Trace Sun Pattern onto yellow construction paper and cut out—one sun for each child. Draw a cloud pattern, 14×17 inches (35×42.5 cm) on butcher paper and cut out. Using pattern, trace clouds onto additional butcher paper and cut out—two clouds for each child. Cut crepe-paper streamers into 18-inch (45-cm) lengths—one length of each color for each child. Cut yarn into 16-inch (40-cm) lengths—one for each child.

Instruct each child in the following procedures:
- Color paper clouds with blue crayon.
- Lay one paper cloud with colored side down onto work surface.
- Glue one end of each crepe-paper streamer across bottom of cloud in rainbow-color order (red, orange, yellow, green, blue and purple [sketch a]).
- Lay the second cloud, colored side down, onto work surface and apply glue around the edge of the cloud, leaving a 6-inch (15-cm) opening near the top (sketch b).
- Place the glued cloud on top of the cloud with streamers, glued side down, making sure edges are even. Press edges together firmly (sketch b).

- Scrunch up three or four paper towels and gently stuff into the opening near the top of cloud.
- Glue opening closed.
- Glue paper sun onto top corner of cloud.
- Punch two holes near the top of the cloud, about 4 inches (10 cm) apart. Thread yarn through holes for hanging and tie a knot at ends (sketch c). Trim ends if needed.

Simplification Idea: Teacher uses stapler to staple edges of clouds together for children.

Bible Bits: **You can hang your Noah's Rain Cloud near an open window to see the rainbow streamers flutter in the wind. When have you seen a real rainbow?** (Children respond.) **God made the rainbow in the sky to remind us that He loves us and will never send another flood to cover the earth.**

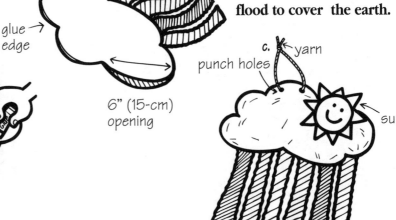

b.

glue edge →

6" (15-cm) opening

c. yarn

punch holes

sun

a.

SUN PATTERN

NOAH'S FLOOD MUD MAT
(15-20 MINUTES)

Materials
- dry soil
- brown and blue liquid tempera paint
- heavyweight muslin
- wire mesh strainer or window screen
- small coffee cans
- animal-shaped sponges
- paint-stirring sticks
- pinking shears
- measuring cups

Standard Supplies
- measuring stick
- shallow containers
- newspaper
- water

Preparation: Gather 1 cup of soil for every four children in class. With pinking shears, cut muslin into 12×18-inch (30×45-cm) mats—one for each child. Cover work area with newspaper.

Instruct each child in the following procedures:
- Have children form groups of four. With adult help, children take turns shaking dirt through wire screen into coffee can until they have ½ cup fine dirt.
- Add ¼ cup paint to fine dirt and stir until smooth. (Add a small amount of water if mixture seems too dry or becomes dry while sponging.)
- Pour paints into shallow containers.
- Dip animal sponges into paint and press onto mat.
- Let dry overnight.

Bible Bits: What happens to dirt outside when it rains? (It becomes mud.) **After the rain stopped and Noah and the animals got out of the ark, the earth must have been very muddy! What animals can you name that went in the ark? What animals did you print on your mud mat?**

"STARS IN THE SKY" MOBILE

(15-20 MINUTES)

Materials

- Star Patterns
- sand
- string

For each child—

- one blue plastic clothes hanger

Standard Supplies

- photocopier
- yellow construction paper or card stock
- glitter crayons
- glue
- transparent tape
- scissors
- measuring stick
- shallow containers
- large shallow box

Preparation: Photocopy Star Patterns onto card stock or construction paper—two copies for each child. Cut out stars. (Older children may cut out their own stars.) For each child—cut string into three 18-inch (45-cm) lengths and two 30-inch (75-cm) lengths and tie onto the bottom bar of clothes hanger. Trim ends, if needed. Pour sand into shallow containers.

Instruct each child in the following procedures:

- Color some stars with glitter crayons.
- On other stars, dot with glue and then sprinkle with sand. Shake off excess sand into the shallow box.
- With teacher's help, tape the backs of stars to the strings (see sketch). Tape one, two or three stars to each string.

Bible Bits: How many stars do you think there are in the sky? (Children respond.) **There are so many we cannot even count them! God promised Abraham he would have as many children, grandchildren and great grandchildren as there are stars in the sky! God kept His promises. Your Stars in the Sky Mobile will remind you that God keeps His promises!**

STAR PATTERNS

DREAMING JOSEPH PUPPET
(15-20 MINUTES)

Materials
- Joseph's Coat Pattern
- tempera paint in various colors

For each child—
- one small brown paper bag

Standard Supplies
- photocopier
- white card stock
- felt pens
- craft glue
- paintbrushes
- scissors
- shallow containers
- newspaper

Preparation: Photocopy Joseph's Coat Pattern onto card stock and cut out—one for each child. Cover work area with newspaper. Pour paint into shallow containers.

Instruct each child in the following procedures:
- Paint Joseph's coat with various colors. Set aside to dry.
- Lay bag with the bottom facing up. Draw two closed eyes with eyelashes on the bottom of the bag (sketch a).
- Bend the bottom of bag back. On the bag under the flap, draw eyes that are open (sketch b). Below the eyes draw a nose and mouth. (Teacher may have to draw face on puppet for younger children.)
- Glue the painted coat onto bag under Joseph's face (sketch c).
- When puppet is dry, put your hand in the paper bag. Close the bottom flap to make Joseph sleep and dream. Open the flap to make him wake up!

Bible Bits: **What colors did you paint Joseph's coat, (Adam)? Joseph's father gave him a special coat. How did his brothers feel toward Joseph?** (They were jealous and angry.) **Sometimes we are jealous when someone gets something that we want or gets to do something special that we'd like to do. But instead of being angry, God wants us to be happy for other people.**

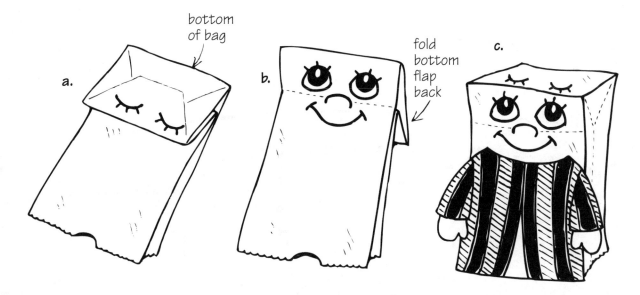

bottom of bag

a.

b.

fold bottom flap back

c.

JOSEPH'S COAT PATTERN

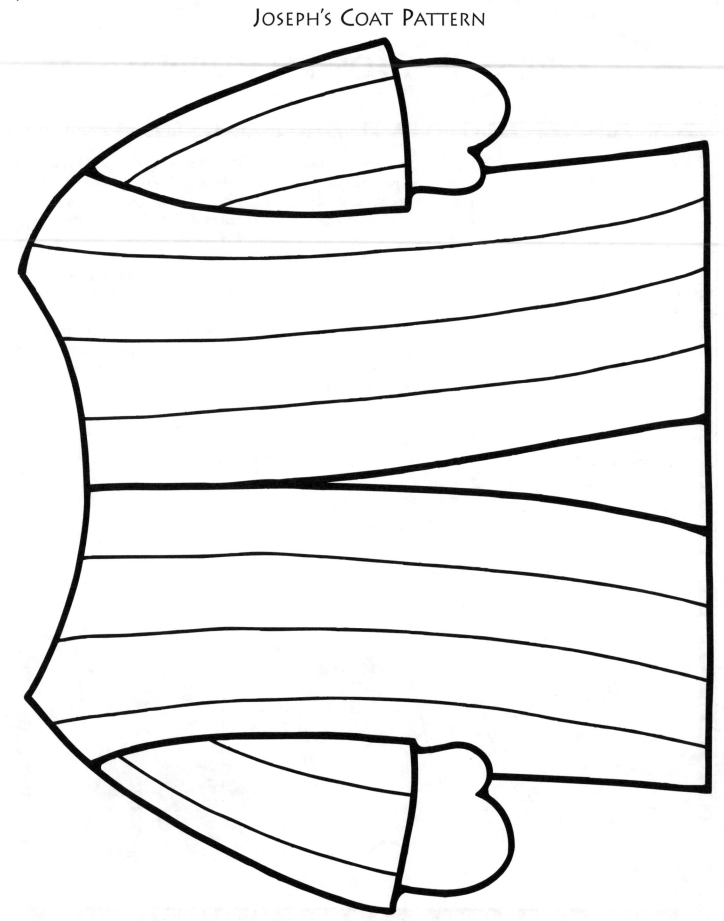

BABY MOSES IN A BASKET

(15-20 MINUTES)

Materials
◆ peach-colored felt
◆ fiberfill stuffing
◆ raffia or straw
◆ black permanent felt pens

For each child—
◆ one toilet-paper tube
◆ one white baby sock
◆ one small rubber band

Standard Supplies
◆ yellow or tan construction paper
◆ glue
◆ scissors
◆ measuring stick

Preparation: Cut felt into 1½-inch (3.75-cm) circles—one for each child. Cut out a ½-inch (1.25-cm) strip of each toilet-paper tube as shown in sketch a. Cut construction paper into 1×13-inch strips (2.5×32.5-cm)—one for each child.

Instruct each child in the following procedures:
◆ Use felt pen to draw a baby face on felt circle.
◆ Fill baby sock with stuffing almost to the top.
◆ With teacher's help, secure rubber band around top of sock as shown in sketch b.
◆ Glue face on sock directly below rubber band (sketch c).
◆ Fold top of sock down to make cap (sketch d).
◆ Spread glue on the construction paper strip.
◆ Glue construction paper strip around toilet-paper tube to make basket (sketch e).
◆ Glue pieces of straw or raffia on basket.
◆ Place Baby Moses in his basket after glue dries.

Bible Bits: Miriam did something very special. Miriam had a baby brother named Moses. Miriam's mother had to hide Moses in a basket because mean Pharaoh wanted to kill all the baby boys in Egypt. Miriam's mother put Moses in a little basket boat and hid it by the river's edge. Miriam was brave and stayed to watch over her baby brother. God made Miriam special. God made you special, too. What is something special you can do to help your mom?

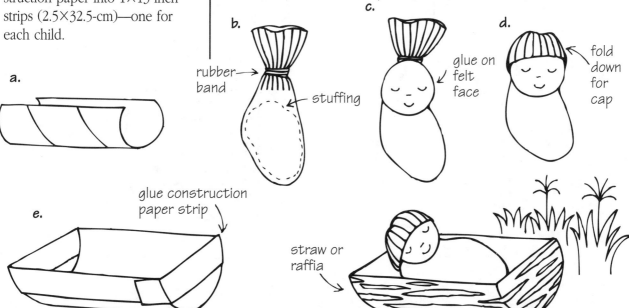

a.

b.
rubber band → ← stuffing

c. glue on felt face →

d. fold down for cap →

e. glue construction paper strip →

straw or raffia →

SALTY SEA JAR
(20-30 MINUTES)

Materials
- table salt
- spray paint
- green and blue powdered tempera paint
- cotton balls
- spoons
- three plastic margarine tubs with lids
- measuring cups and spoons

For each child—
- one clean baby-food jar with lid

Standard Supplies
- craft glue
- newspaper

Preparation: In a well-ventilated area, cover surface with newspaper and spray paint jar lids. Pour 1 cup salt in a margarine tub. In other margarine tubs, mix 1 cup salt with 1 teaspoon tempera for each color. (Three cups of salt will fill six baby food jars.) Place spoon in each tub.

Instruct each child in the following procedures:
- With spoon, layer green salt in bottom of baby food jar (sketch a).
- Add a blue layer of salt.
- Add a white layer of salt.
- Repeat layering until jar is filled.
- Tap jar lightly to let salt settle.
- Place several cotton balls on top of salt.
- Teacher squeezes glue around jar rim and tightly screws on lid (sketch b).

Enrichment Idea: Have children help mix tempera and salt. Measure ingredients, snap lid on margarine tubs, and have children shake the mixture to color the salt.

Bible Bits: **When Moses and the Israelites left Egypt, Pharaoh chased after them to bring them back. Suddenly Moses and the people came to a big sea. They couldn't go any further. But God helped Moses. What did God do?** (He sent a great wind to blow back the water of the sea. Moses and the people crossed the sea on a dry path.) **Everyone was safe on the other side. Then God closed up the sea. God kept everyone safe!**

a.

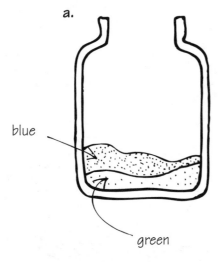

blue

green

b.

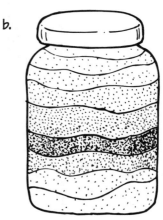

DESERT SAND PAINTING
(10-15 MINUTES)

Materials
- sand
- large shallow box
- several spoons

Standard Supplies
- brown construction paper
- orange and yellow crayons
- glue
- paintbrushes
- shallow containers

Preparation: Pour glue into shallow containers. Pour sand into other shallow containers.

Instruct each child in the following procedures:
- Near the top of the paper, use orange and yellow crayons to draw and color a sun (sketch a).
- Use paintbrush to paint glue on the paper to make mountains and the desert ground.
- Place your picture in the shallow box. Use a spoon to sprinkle sand over the glue.
- Carefully shake off the extra sand from your picture into the box (sketch b).
- Lay picture flat to dry.

Bible Bits: The desert is hot and dry. Moses and the Israelites lived in the desert for a long, long time. But God took care of them. He sent food for them to eat. He gave them water to drink. Even though sometimes the people disobeyed Him, God still loved them and took care of them. How does God take care of you?

a. draw sun

b.

sand

"PART THE WATER" PICTURE
(20-25 MINUTES)

Materials
- tan and blue acrylic paint
- sponges
- clothespins (spring-type)
- colored dot stickers
- yarn

For each child—
- one 8½×11-inch (21.5×27.5-cm) sheet of white card stock
- one overhead transparency

Standard Supplies
- brown and orange construction paper
- fine-tip felt pens
- pencils
- glue sticks
- scissors
- hole punch
- ruler
- shallow containers
- water
- newspaper

Preparation: Draw a pencil line horizontally across the center of each sheet of card stock and transparency (sketch a). Cut brown construction paper into wavy mountain range shape approximately 2×11 inches (5×27.5 cm)—one for each child (sketch b). Cut orange construction paper into 1½-inch (3.75-cm) circles—one for each child. Dampen sponges and cut into small squares—one for each child. Clip a clothespin to each sponge. Cover work area with newspaper. Pour paint into shallow containers.

Instruct each child in the following procedures:
- Use tan paint to sponge paint bottom half of white card stock (sketch c).
- Use blue paint to sponge paint bottom half of transparency. Allow paint to dry.
- Glue the mountain range above tan section on card stock (sketch d).
- Glue the orange sun above the mountains.
- Stick dot stickers in the middle of tan section to represent the Israelites crossing the dry ground. Draw faces on dots with felt pens.
- Lay transparency on top of paper so that the blue paint is covering the tan paint. With teacher's help, punch four evenly spaced holes along both sides of card stock and transparency (sketch e).
- Insert yarn through first hole and tie a knot. Thread yarn through remaining holes as shown in sketch e and tie another knot to secure. Repeat process for opposite edge of picture.
- Use scissors to cut transparency in half vertically (sketch f).
- Open and close the top sheet to show how God parted the Red Sea and allowed the Israelites to cross on dry ground (sketch g).

Simplification Idea: Use Bible character stickers for Moses and the Israelites.

Bible Bits: **God took care of the Israelites when they escaped from Egypt. He wanted them to travel safely to a new home. How did God help them escape when they reached the Red Sea?** (God sent a big wind that blew the sea back. Then the people could walk across to the other side.) **What do you think the Israelites said after God helped them escape?**

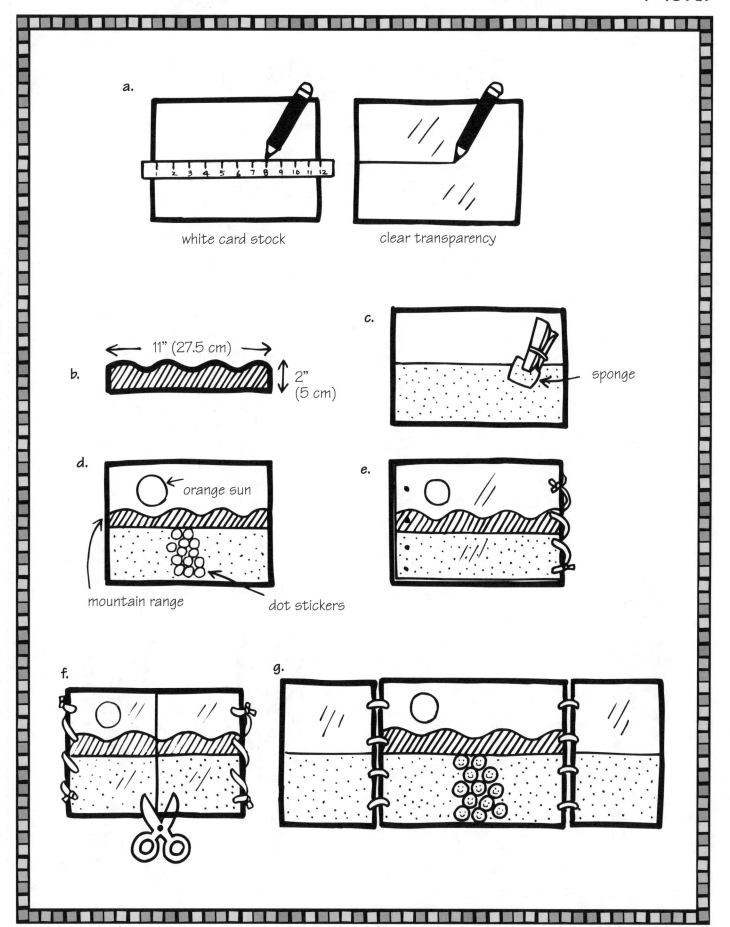

a.

white card stock   clear transparency

b. ← 11" (27.5 cm) →   2" (5 cm)

c. sponge

d. orange sun
mountain range   dot stickers

e.

f.

g.

The Big Book of Bible Crafts

GIDEON'S TORCH
(15-20 MINUTES)

Materials
- tissue paper in red, yellow and orange
- gold or other metallic-colored crayons

Standard Supplies
- black construction paper
- glue
- transparent tape
- scissors
- paintbrushes
- shallow containers
- ruler

Preparation: Cut tissue paper into 12-inch (30-cm) squares—four to five squares for each child. Pour glue into shallow containers.

Instruct each child in the following procedures:
- Decorate the black paper with gold or metallic-colored crayons.
- With teacher's help, roll the paper (colored side out) into a narrow cone-shape. Tape edges in place (sketch a).
- To make tissue flames, place a crayon in the center of a tissue square. Gather the tissue around the end of crayon. Remove the crayon and pinch the gathered end of tissue together (sketch b).
- Brush glue on the inside edge of paper torch.
- Place the end of tissue paper flame on the glued part of torch (sketch c).
- Repeat to make additional flames and glue to torch (sketch d).
- Allow to dry.

Bible Bits: In Bible times, people didn't have lights to turn on in the dark. They needed candles or fire to see at night. God told Gideon to have his army hide their torches under clay jars, so the enemy couldn't see them in the dark. What happened when Gideon's army broke their jars? (The light shone through and surprised the enemy.) **Then Gideon's men blew their trumpets. The enemy was so scared, they ran away. Because Gideon obeyed God, he won the battle without fighting!**

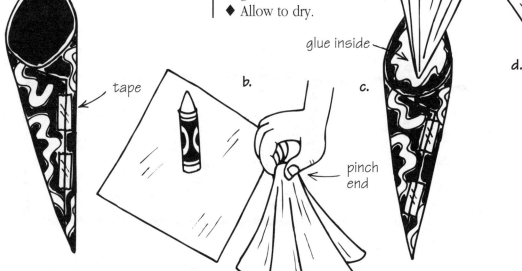

a.

tape

b.

pinch end

c.

glue inside

d.

PRAISE SHAKER
(15-20 MINUTES)

Materials
- corrugated cardboard
- dried beans
- liquid tempera paints in various colors

For each child—
- one tennis-ball canister or potato-chip canister with lid
- one tree leaf

Standard Supplies
- white construction paper
- glue
- paintbrushes
- scissors
- shallow containers
- newspaper

Preparation: Cut construction paper to fit around each canister. Cut cardboard into squares larger than each leaf—one for each child. Glue smooth side of each leaf onto cardboard square and allow glue to dry (sketch a). Cover work area with newspaper. Pour paint into shallow containers.

Instruct each child in the following procedures:
- With paintbrush, spread a thin coat of paint onto leaf.
- Press painted side of leaf onto construction paper. Carefully lift off leaf (sketch b).
- Repeat printing process several times to make a design. Let dry.
- Place several beans inside canister and glue on plastic lid.
- Glue decorated paper onto canister (sketch c). Allow to dry.

Enrichment Idea: Older children can glue leaves onto cardboard to make their own printing blocks.

Bible Bits: **David loved to make music and sing to God just like we do. He told God he loved Him and thanked Him for taking care of him. This is called praising God. You can use your Praise Shaker when you sing songs to God.**

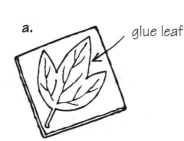

a.

glue leaf

b.

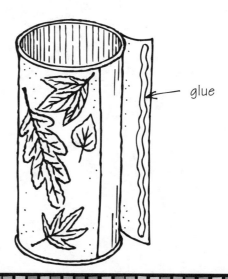

c.

glue

DAVID'S HARP
(10-15 MINUTES)

Materials
- Harp Pattern
- corrugated cardboard
- drinking straws

For each child—
- five 3-inch (7.5-cm) rubber bands

Standard Supplies
- wide-tip felt pens
- pencil
- transparent tape
- heavy-duty scissors
- ruler

Preparation: Trace Harp Pattern onto cardboard and cut out—one for each child. Cut straws into 4-inch (10-cm) pieces—one for each child.

Instruct each child in the following procedures:
- Color cardboard pieces with felt pens to decorate.
- Tape straw piece across harp, 1 inch (2.5 cm) from the top edge.
- Stretch the five rubber bands over cardboard and straw to make harp strings (see sketch).
- When completed, pluck the strings of your harp to play music like David!

Bible Bits: (Monique), you can make pretty sounds with your harp. What are some songs you like to sing? (Child responds.) There are lots of songs we can sing to God. When we sing songs to God, we are praising Him. To praise someone is to say how good he is. David liked to sing and praise God with his harp.

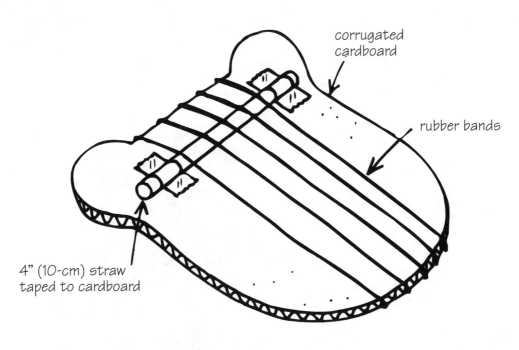

corrugated cardboard

rubber bands

4" (10-cm) straw taped to cardboard

HARP PATTERN

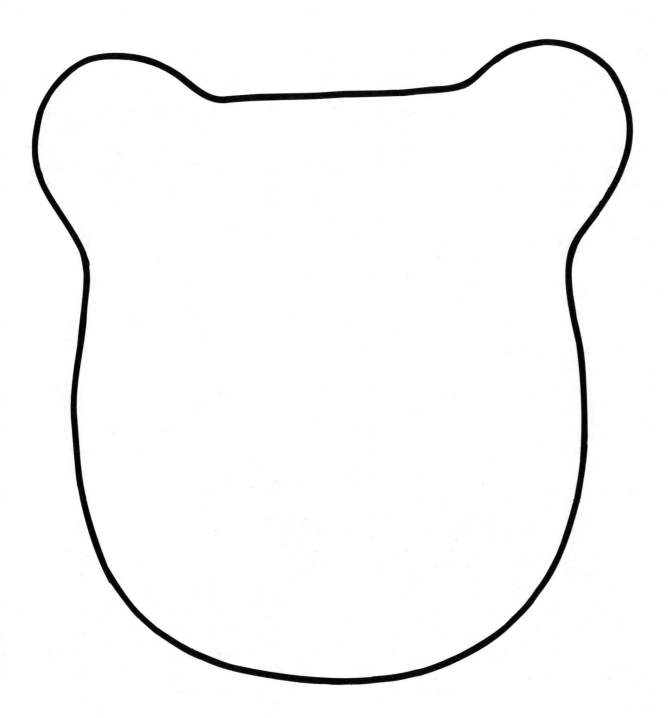

FUZZY LAMB
(25-30 MINUTES)

Materials
- Ear Pattern
- cotton balls
- white felt
- black chenille wire

For each child—
- white paper plate
- black medium-sized pom-pom
- two wiggle eyes

Standard Supplies
- pencils
- glue
- scissors
- ruler

Preparation: Trace Ear Pattern onto white felt—two ears for each child. Cut out ears. Cut chenille wire into 4-inch (10-cm) lengths.

Instruct each child in the following procedures:
- Cut through the rim of the paper plate at approximately 1-inch (2.5-cm) intervals.
- Using a pencil, curl back the paper-plate fringe (sketch a). (Younger children may need help with curling the fringe.)
- Glue one felt ear to each side of plate edge.
- Glue cotton balls to front center of plate to cover.
- Glue on black pom-pom for nose, chenille wire piece for mouth and wiggle eyes to complete lamb's face.

Bible Bits: David loved and took care of his sheep. Do you have an animal to take care of? How do you show love to your pet? God wants us to show love to animals and especially to each other. How could you show love to your friends? This Fuzzy Lamb will help you remember to show love to others.

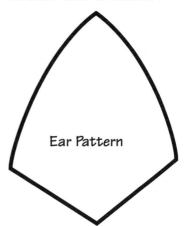

Ear Pattern

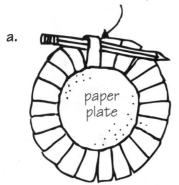

curl around pencil

a.

paper plate

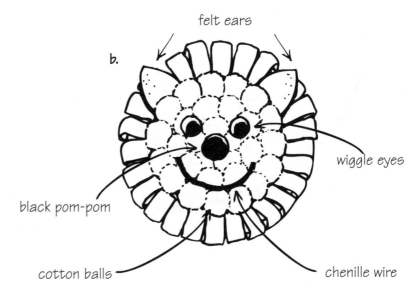

b.

felt ears

wiggle eyes

black pom-pom

cotton balls

chenille wire

LIL' WORKER'S APRON
(15-20 MINUTES)

Materials
- Tool Patterns
- muslin fabric
- ¼-inch (.625-cm) bias tape
- sewing machine and thread
- felt pens or squeeze bottles of fabric paints in various colors
- tongue depressors
- safety pin

Standard Supplies
- photocopier
- colored card stock
- glue
- fabric scissors
- scissors
- measuring stick

Preparation: Photocopy Tool Patterns onto card stock—one sheet for each child. Make a tool apron for each child according to the following directions: Use fabric scissors to cut a 10×12-inch (25×30-cm) rectangle out of muslin. Sew a ½-inch (1.25-cm) hem on both short sides and one long side of fabric (sketch a). Fold up the hemmed long side of fabric to make a 4-inch (10-cm) pocket as shown in sketch b. Sew pocket along sides; then stitch down the middle of pocket to make two smaller pockets. Fold down the top edge of apron ½-inch (1.25-cm) and sew along edge to make casing. Pin safety pin to one end of a 3-foot (.9-m) length of bias tape and thread through casing (sketch c).

Instruct each child in the following procedures:
- Cut out card-stock tools.
- Glue a tongue depressor to the back of each tool to make sturdy (sketch d).
- Decorate apron using felt pens or squeeze bottles of fabric paint (sketch e). Allow to dry.
- Put tools in your apron pockets and with teacher's help, tie apron around waist.

Simplification Idea: For younger children, teacher cuts out card-stock tools.

Bible Bits: In Bible times, it took lots of people to help build God's Temple. There were workers who cut the stones for the steps. There were woodcutters who cut the trees for the walls. There were metalworkers who made beautiful things out of gold and bronze. Everyone worked together. If you were helping to build the Temple, what work would you like to do, (Eric)? What jobs do you like to do at home? You can wear your apron when you work at home with your family.

a.

½" (1.25 cm) hem

10" (25 cm)

12" (30 cm)

b.

2" (5 cm)

4" (10 cm)

front of apron

c.

½" (1.25 cm) casing

safety pin

back of apron

d. glue tongue depressor to back

e.

TOOL PATTERNS

RAVEN PUPPET
(15-20 MINUTES)

Materials
- Raven Pattern
- black feathers
- small stale pieces of bread

For each child—
- two wiggle eyes
- one drinking straw

Standard Supplies
- small sheets of black construction paper
- pencil
- craft glue
- transparent tape
- scissors

Preparation: Fold construction paper in half, place Raven Pattern on fold and trace pattern (sketch a)—one for each child. Cut out ravens.

Instruct each child in the following procedures:
- Fold down the wings of your raven to make them stick out (sketch b).
- Glue the bird's body together (sketch b). Don't glue the wings.
- Tape a drinking straw to the middle of the body, under the wings.
- Glue feathers onto the top of wings.
- Glue one wiggle eye on each side of head.
- Glue a small piece of bread to the raven's beak.

- Allow glue to dry; then hold onto the straw and move it up and down to make your Raven Puppet fly!

Bible Bits: **What happens if there is no rain for a long time?** (Nothing grows. Streams dry up.) **Where Elijah lived, it hadn't rained for a long time, so there was little food and water. But God helped Elijah find a stream that had water. He sent the ravens to give Elijah food. God took care of Elijah. How does God take care of you?**

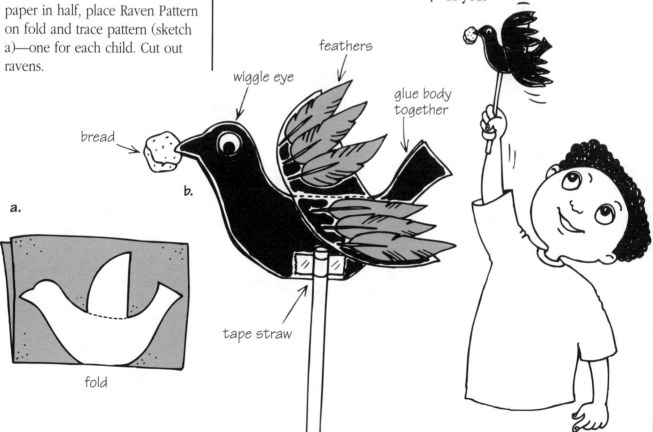

bread

wiggle eye

feathers

glue body together

a.

b.

tape straw

fold

Raven Pattern

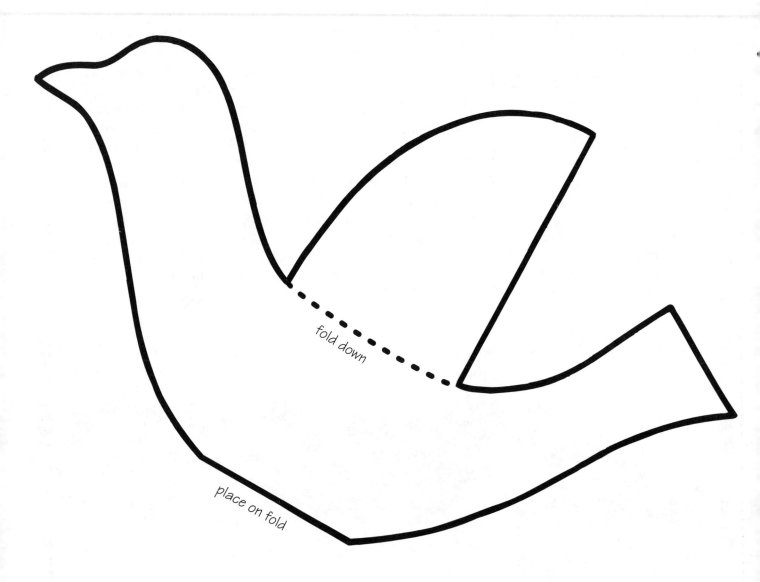

fold down

place on fold

"THREE MEN IN A FIRE" STICK PUPPETS
(25-30 MINUTES)

Materials
- red and orange food coloring
- fabric and felt scraps
- pinking shears

For each child—
- three tongue depressors
- one plastic straw
- six small wiggle eyes
- three mini pom-poms

Standard Supplies
- yellow card stock
- fine-tip felt pens
- glue
- transparent tape
- scissors
- ruler
- newspaper

Preparation: Cut fabric and felt scraps into 2-inch (5-cm) squares—three for each child. Cut card stock into 7-inch (17.5-cm) squares—one for every two children. Fold squares in half diagonally. Use pinking shears to cut square into two equal triangles (sketch a). Cover work area with newspaper.

Instruct each child in the following procedures:
- Teacher puts a drop of red and orange food coloring on bottom corner of card-stock triangle. Child quickly blows through straw to spread the color. Repeat if desired. Allow to dry.
- To make Shadrach, Meshach and Abednego, glue two wiggle eyes onto each of the three tongue depressors (sketch b). Glue on pom-poms for noses.
- Use felt pens to draw hair, headband and other features on figures.
- Wrap and glue fabric and/or felt squares around puppets to make clothes.
- Fold paper into a cone shape (sketch c). Tape edges closed.
- Place puppets in cone pocket to show Shadrach, Meshach and Abednego in the fiery furnace (sketch d).

Simplification Idea: Draw eyes and nose instead of using wiggle eyes and pom-poms.

Enrichment Idea: Children cut tiny pieces of yarn and glue them onto puppets for hair and beards.

Bible Bits: **Shadrach, Meshach and Abednego loved God. They wanted to obey Him. How did they obey God?** (They worshiped only God. They wouldn't bow down to the king's statue.) **How did God save them from the fiery furnace?** (He sent an angel in the fire to protect them.) **How can we show our love to God?** (Pray to Him. Sing. Go to Sunday School to learn about Him. Be kind and loving to other people.)

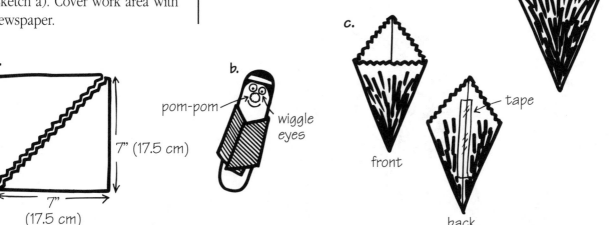

LION PUZZLE MAGNET

(15-20 MINUTES)

Materials
- Lion Pattern
- yellow poster board
- small jigsaw-puzzle pieces
- brown and orange spray paint
- black permanent felt pens
- self-adhesive magnet strips
- one plastic milk jug lid

For each child—
- two 7-mm wiggle eyes

Standard Supplies
- pencil
- craft glue
- scissors
- newspaper
- ruler

Preparation: In well-ventilated area, place puzzle pieces on newspaper and spray paint puzzle pieces orange and brown—approximately 12 total pieces for each child. Trace Lion Pattern onto poster board and cut out—one for each child. Using plastic lid as a pattern, draw a circle for the face of each poster-board lion (sketch a). Cut magnet strips into 3-inch (7.5-cm) lengths—one for each child. Cut triangular tips off some puzzle pieces to use for each lion tail—one tip for each child (sketch b).

Instruct each child in the following procedures:
- Glue wiggle eyes on the lion's face.
- With felt pen, draw nose, mouth, whiskers, legs, toes and tail (sketch c).
- Glue puzzle pieces around face to make mane.
- Glue triangular tip on end of tail.
- Attach a magnet strip to back.

Simplification Idea: Teacher draws lion face and toes or photocopies Lion Pattern onto yellow card stock.

Bible Bits: The lion is very strong and powerful. But God is even more powerful than a lion. God kept Daniel safe in the lions' den. God keeps you safe, too. He gives you people to take care of you. (Michelle), who are the people who care for you?

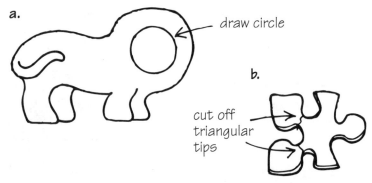

a.

draw circle

b.

cut off triangular tips

c. puzzle tip

puzzle pieces

LION PATTERN

The Big Book of Bible Crafts 41

SPOUTING WHALE
(25-30 MINUTES)

Materials
- Whale Patterns
- tempera paints in black, gray, light blue and green
- small sponge pieces
- clothespins (spring-type)

For each child—
- two paper fasteners
- one medium-sized wiggle eye

Standard Supplies
- white poster board
- pencil
- glue
- scissors
- hole punch
- shallow containers
- newspaper

Preparation: Trace Whale Patterns onto poster board and cut out—one set of patterns for each child. With hole punch, punch holes in each whale piece where indicated on patterns. Cover work area with newspaper. Pour paint in shallow containers. Clip clothespins to sponge pieces to use as handles.

Instruct each child in the following procedures:
- Sponge black paint onto whale body and tail. Then sponge gray paint on top of black paint.
- Sponge blue and green paint on spout.
- Allow to dry.
- Push a paper fastener through the holes in the whale body and the tail to attach tail. Then attach spout to the top of whale with the second paper fastener (see sketch).
- Glue on a wiggle eye.
- Wiggle your whale's tail. Make the water spout move up and down!

Bible Bits: The Bible says a big fish swallowed Jonah. It could have been a whale. Have you ever seen a real whale? God made whales with something special. They have a blow hole on top of their heads. When they come up out of the water, they blow air and water out of their blow holes. The water spouts out like a water sprinkler!

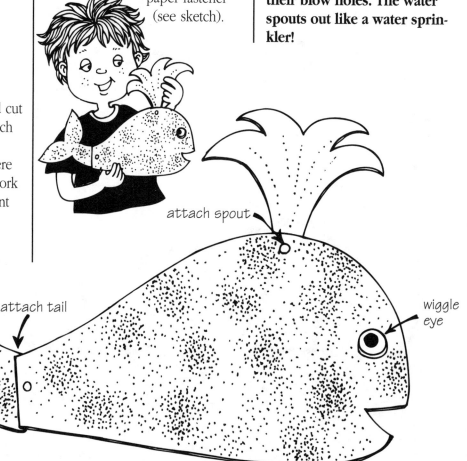

attach spout

attach tail

wiggle eye

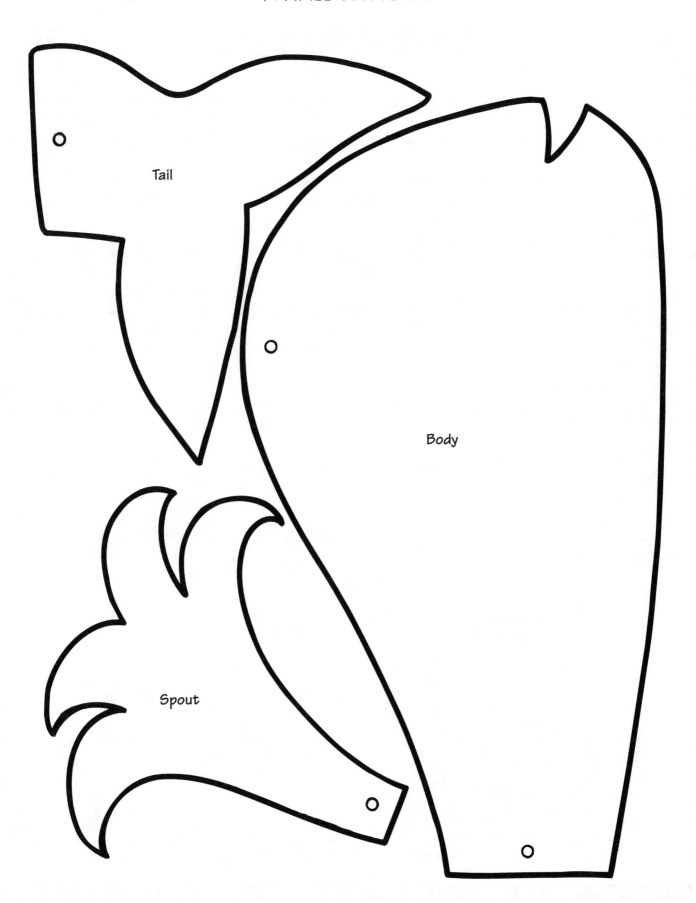

Tail

Body

Spout

JONAH SHAKER
(10-15 MINUTES)

Materials
- Jonah and Fish Patterns
- white or blue plastic disposable plates
- plastic fish-shaped confetti
- blue and green food coloring
- blue electrical tape
- small fish or seashell stickers
- pitcher
- permanent felt pens

For each child—
- one small, clear plastic beverage bottle with cap

Standard Supplies
- scissors
- shallow containers
- water

Preparation: Trace patterns onto plastic plates and cut out—one Jonah and one fish for each child. Fill pitcher with water. Put confetti in shallow containers.

Instruct each child in the following procedures:
- Use permanent felt pens to decorate plastic fish and Jonah.
- Gently bend fish to fit through bottle opening and push fish into bottle. Put Jonah into bottle.
- Drop several confetti fish into bottle.
- With teacher's help, fill bottle with water, stopping 1 inch (2.5 cm) from the top.

- To make the ocean, put a few drops of blue or green food coloring into water. Or mix blue and green food coloring together.
- Put cap on bottle and twist tightly to close.
- Wrap a piece of tape around bottle cap to secure (sketch a).
- Shake bottle to mix food coloring with water.
- Put a few stickers on outside of bottle.
- Tip bottle back and forth to see Jonah and the fish swim under the sea (sketch b).

Bible Bits: **What did God send to swallow Jonah and keep him safe in the ocean?** (A big fish.) **God loved Jonah and took care of him even though Jonah ran away and didn't obey God. God loves you, too. What are some ways God takes care of you?**

a. wrap tape

b.

Jonah Pattern

Fish Pattern

PAPER-PLATE ANGEL
(15-20 MINUTES)

Materials
- white paper plates
- small gold or white doilies
- star stickers
- yarn
- curly doll hair
- glitter

Standard Supplies
- crayons
- glue
- transparent tape
- scissors
- stapler and staples
- hole punch
- ruler

Preparation: Cut angel from paper plate as shown in sketch a—one for each child. Cut yarn into 12-inch (30-cm) lengths. Cut doll hair into short lengths.

Instruct each child in the following procedures:
- With plate facing up, draw face on angel (sketch b).
- Color the portion of the plate below the head to make robe.
- Turn plate over and color the bottom portion of the back side of paper plate to decorate robe.
- With teacher's help, bend robe portion of plate to overlap in front and staple in place (sketch b).
- With teacher's help, bend wings down and tape or staple to back of robe.
- Glue doily behind head for halo, and stick stars onto robe (sketch c).
- With teacher's help, punch hole in top of head. Thread yarn through hole and tie.
- Glue a small amount of curly doll hair to head.
- Spread glue on wings, sprinkle wings with glitter and shake off excess glitter.
- Hang angel and let it fly in the breeze!

Bible Bits: **Angels are God's special messengers. What did the angel tell Mary?** (That Jesus would be born.) **What did angels tell the shepherds?** (That Jesus was born.) **Jesus was born as a baby. Later when He grew up, He told everyone about God and His love for us.**

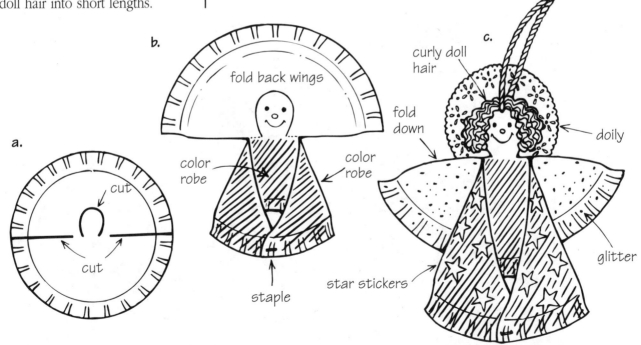

b.

fold back wings

color robe

color robe

staple

a.

cut

cut

c.

curly doll hair

fold down

doily

star stickers

glitter

THE BABY JESUS DOLL
(10-15 MINUTES)

Materials
- fabric
- tongue depressors
- yarn
- small cardboard jewelry boxes (type used for earrings)
- straw or dried grass

Standard Supplies
- fine-tip felt pens
- glue
- scissors
- ruler

Preparation: Cut fabric into 2-inch (5-cm) squares. Cut tongue depressors to fit inside jewelry box. Cut yarn into small pieces.

Instruct each child in the following procedures:
- Spread glue on one side of the rounded edge of tongue depressor (sketch a).
- Press yarn pieces onto glue to make hair (sketch b).
- Glue straw or dried grass to the inside of small jewelry box.
- Use felt pens to draw facial features on the tongue-depressor doll (sketch b).
- Place tongue depressor doll in straw and cover with fabric piece (sketch c).

Simplification Idea: Teacher draws facial features on tongue depressor.

Enrichment Idea: Children use crayons to decorate box.

Bible Bits: **What is the name of God's Son? Where was Jesus born?** (In a stable.) **Jesus' mother put the baby Jesus in a manger filled with hay. Jesus came to earth as a baby, and then He grew to be a man. Jesus came to tell people about God's love.**

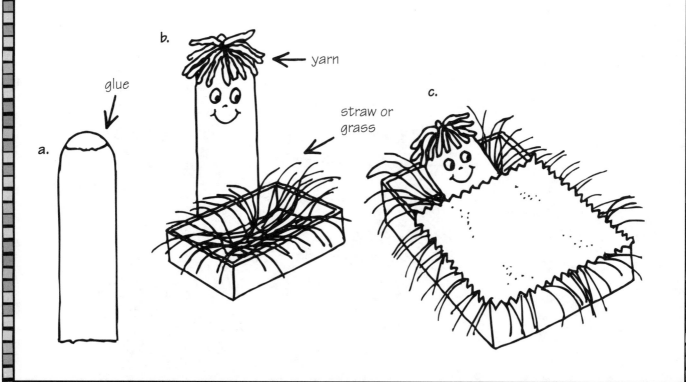

glue

a.

b.

yarn

straw or grass

c.

MARY AND JOSEPH MANGER SCENE
(15-20 MINUTES)

Materials
- Manger Scene Patterns
- Fun Foam or colored paper in light blue, dark blue, pink and brown
- fabric scraps
- yellow tissue paper

For each child—
- four tongue depressors

Standard Supplies
- 8½×11-inch (21.5×27.5-cm) sheets of purple card stock
- pen
- brown crayons or felt pens
- glue
- scissors
- ruler

Preparation: Trace Head Pattern onto pink Fun Foam or colored paper and cut out—two for each child. Trace Body Pattern onto dark and light blue Fun Foam or paper and cut out—one of each for each child. Trace Manger Pattern onto brown Fun Foam or paper and cut out—one for each child. Trace Head Covering Pattern onto fabric scraps and cut out—two for each child. Cut tissue paper into 5-inch (12.5-cm) squares—one for each child.

Instruct each child in the following procedures:
- Color four tongue depressors with brown crayons or felt pens.
- Lay the purple card stock horizontally. Glue two tongue depressors near the top edge to make the stable's roof (see sketch).
- Glue a tongue depressor onto each side of card stock to make the stable's walls.
- Glue the brown piece of foam or paper in the center bottom of the stable to make the manger.
- Crumple tissue square and glue to the top of manger for hay.

- Glue one triangle body piece on each side of manger to make Mary and Joseph (see sketch).
- Glue head circles on top of triangle bodies.
- Glue fabric onto heads to make head coverings.
- Allow glue to dry.

Bible Bits: **Why was Jesus born in a stable?** (Mary and Joseph couldn't find anywhere else to stay.) **Where did baby Jesus sleep?** (In a manger.) **Jesus was God's own Son. Mary and Joseph were glad that God had chosen them to take care of baby Jesus. Do you have a baby at home that you help take care of?**

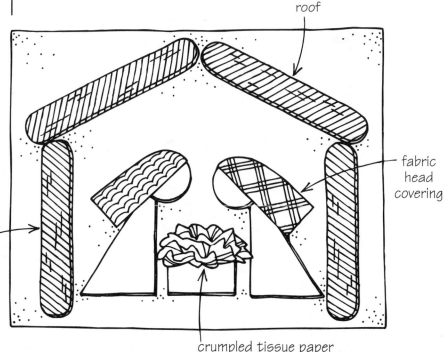

roof

fabric head covering

wall

crumpled tissue paper

MANGER SCENE PATTERNS

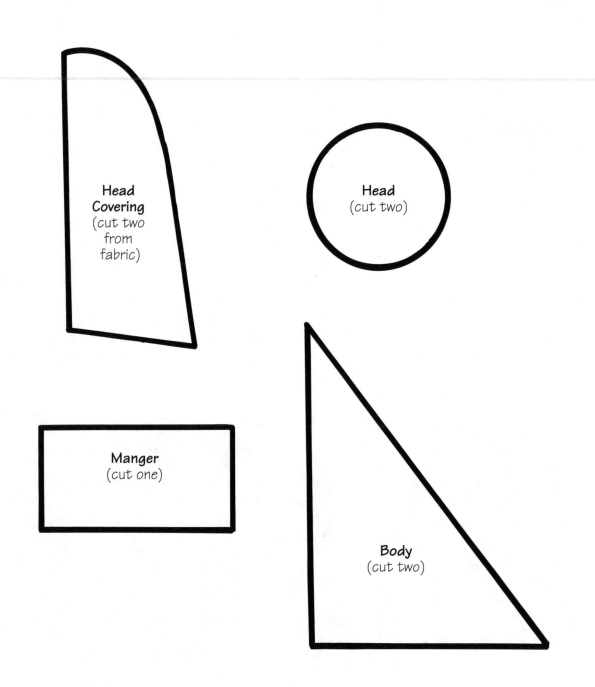

Head Covering
(cut two
from
fabric)

Head
(cut two)

Manger
(cut one)

Body
(cut two)

"JESUS IS BORN" STAINED-GLASS PICTURE
(10-15 MINUTES)

Materials
- "Jesus is Born" Picture
- baby oil
- cotton balls

For each child—
- one large magazine

Standard Supplies
- photocopier
- white copier paper
- crayons

Preparation: Photocopy "Jesus is Born" Picture onto white paper— one copy for each child.

Instruct each child in the following procedures:
- Color the picture with crayons.
- Lay the picture on top of magazine.
- With teacher's help, apply baby oil to a cotton ball.
- Rub the cotton ball over picture to spread the oil. The oil will make the picture translucent (sketch a).
- Tape your picture to a window and let the light shine through it (sketch b)!

Bible Bits: Jesus was born in a stable. What did the baby Jesus sleep on? (Hay.) What kind of animals do you think were in the stable? Jesus is God's Son. He came to show us God's love.

a.

b.

"For to us a child is born, to us a son is given." Isaiah 9:6

PETER'S BOAT
(10-15 MINUTES)

Materials
- Fun Foam in various colors

For each child—
- one drinking straw
- one 1-inch (2.5-cm) thick household sponge

Standard Supplies
- felt pens
- glue
- hot-glue gun and glue sticks
- scissors
- hole punch
- ruler

Preparation: Cut corners off one end of each sponge (sketch a). In the center of sponge, use tip of scissors to poke a hole large enough for the straw to fit into (sketch a). Cut Fun Foam into 4×6-inch (10×15-cm) rectangles—one for every two children. Then cut rectangles in half diagonally to make two sails (sketch b). Cut additional Fun Foam into small shapes (squares, strips, triangles, etc.). Plug in glue gun out of reach of children.

Instruct each child in the following procedures:
- Use felt pens to decorate sail.
- Glue Fun Foam shapes onto sail for additional decoration.
- With teacher's help, punch a hole at the top and the bottom of sail (sketch c).
- Insert straw through the two holes for the mast. Pull sail to top of straw (sketch d).
- Have teacher use hot-glue gun to glue bottom end of straw into sponge hole (sketch d).

Enrichment Ideas: Teacher writes "Jesus Loves Me!" on a piece of Fun Foam for child to glue onto sail. Provide large containers of shallow water or a water table in which children sail their boats.

Bible Bits: **(Katie), you were patient while you waited for the teacher to glue the sail to your boat. Jesus wants us to be patient with other people. When we are patient with each other, we are showing love to them. Where will you float your boat?**

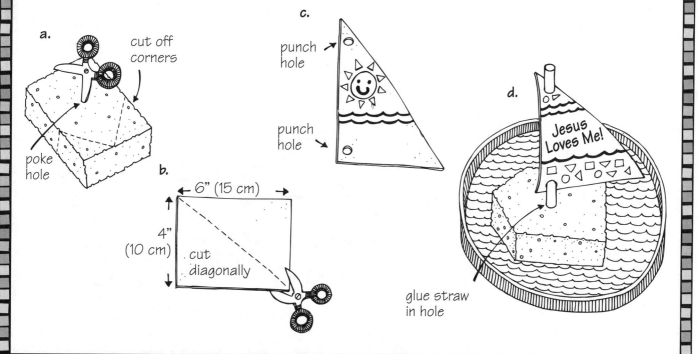

a. cut off corners / poke hole

b. 6" (15 cm) / 4" (10 cm) / cut diagonally

c. punch hole / punch hole

d. Jesus Loves Me! / glue straw in hole

The Big Book of Bible Crafts 51

PAPER-BAG FISH
(20-25 MINUTES)

Materials
- tempera paint in various colors
- newsprint paper
- yarn

For each child—
- one small brown paper bag
- two large wiggle eyes

Standard Supplies
- craft glue
- scissors
- paintbrushes
- shallow containers
- newspaper
- ruler

Preparation: Cut yarn into 6-inch (15-cm) pieces—one for each child. Cover work area with newspaper. Pour paint into shallow containers.

Instruct each child in the following procedures:
- Crumple pieces of newsprint paper and stuff into the bag until it is half full.
- Gather the opening of the bag to make the fish's tail.
- Hold tail together while teacher ties yarn around it (sketch a). Trim yarn ends.
- Paint the entire bag to look like a fish. Decorate with various colors.
- Paint the fish's mouth on the end (bottom) of the bag (sketch b).
- Glue a wiggle eye on each side of paper-bag fish (sketch b). Allow to dry.

Enrichment Idea: When fish are dry, put all the children's fish together in a large fishing net and reenact the story of Jesus calling the fishermen to be His disciples.

Bible Bits: What did Jesus say to the fishermen when He passed by them? (Come and follow me.) Jesus wanted them to become His friends and help Him tell people about God. The fishermen left their fishing boats and fishing nets to go with Jesus. They knew that Jesus was special. Jesus was God's own Son.

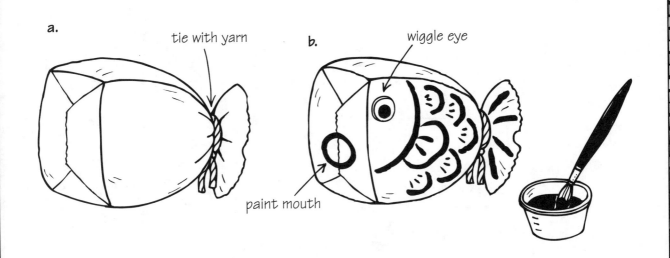

a. tie with yarn

b. wiggle eye

paint mouth

MIRACLE PICTURE
(5-10 MINUTES)

Materials
- powdered drink mixes in various colors
- several empty spice containers with shaker lids
- plastic tub or bucket

Standard Supplies
- white paper sheets
- newspaper
- water

Preparation: Remove plastic shaker lids from each empty spice container. Pour one color of powdered drink mix into each container. Replace shaker lids. Fill plastic tub or bucket with water. Cover work area with a thick layer of newspaper.

Instruct each child in the following procedures:
- Carefully dip your paper into the water to get it wet (sketch a).
- Lay your paper flat on the newspaper.
- Gently sprinkle drink mix from a shaker onto your paper (sketch b). What color appears?
- Shake several colors if you like.
- Keep paper flat to dry.

Enrichment Ideas: Allow children to make several pictures, or use a large piece of butcher paper for all children to make a Miracle Mural.

Bible Bits: (Billy), you can make colors appear on your white sheet of paper. Is that a miracle? (No.) People can do a lot of amazing things, but only God and Jesus can make a real miracle. Jesus performed many miracles to help people. What was the miracle that Jesus did in our Bible story?

HELPER BEE NOTE HOLDER
(10-15 MINUTES)

Materials
- Bee Pattern
- yellow poster board
- ½-inch (1.25-cm) -wide self-adhesive magnetic tape

For each child—
- one clothespin (spring-type)
- one black chenille wire
- two 7-mm wiggle eyes

Standard Supplies
- black crayons or felt pens
- pencil
- glue
- scissors
- ruler

Preparation: Trace Bee Pattern onto yellow poster board and cut out—one for each child. Cut magnetic tape into 3-inch (7.5-cm) lengths—one for each child. Cut each black chenille wire into six ¾-inch (1.9-cm) lengths and two 1½-inch (3.75-cm) lengths.

Instruct each child in the following procedures:
- With a black crayon or felt pen, draw a smile on the bee's face.
- Color black stripes on the bee's body.
- Glue wiggle eyes on bee's face.
- Glue six small black chenille wires to bee's body for legs (sketch a).

- Bend the ends of the two longer black chenille wires to make antennae and glue to bee's head.
- Glue the bee to the top side of clothespin.
- Attach magnet to back of clothespin (sketch b).
- Set aside to allow glue to dry.

Bible Bits: **Your Helper Bee will help papers stay in one place. How did Jesus help someone in our story?** (Child responds.) **Jesus wants us to help other people, too. What are some ways you can help people?**

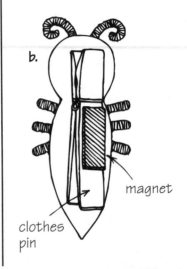

b.

magnet

clothes pin

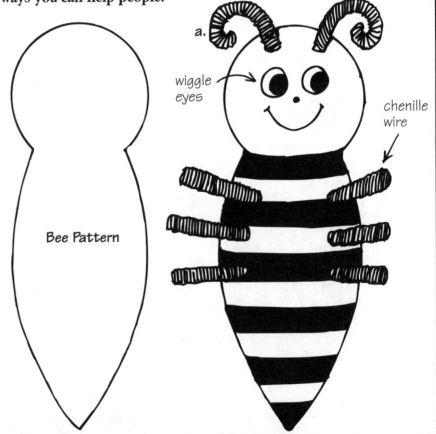

a.

wiggle eyes

chenille wire

Bee Pattern

STAND-UP SYCAMORE TREE
(25-30 MINUTES)

Materials
- Stand-Up Tree Pattern
- green and yellow tissue paper

Standard Supplies
- white poster board
- pencil
- brown crayons
- paintbrushes
- glue
- scissors
- ruler
- shallow containers
- water

Preparation: Trace Stand-Up Tree Pattern onto poster board and cut out—two trees for each child. Cut slit on one tree piece from top to middle and cut slit on other tree piece from bottom to middle as indicated on pattern. Cut or tear tissue paper into 2-inch (5-cm) squares. Pour glue into shallow pans. Dilute glue with water.

Instruct each child in the following procedures:
- Use crayons to color tree trunks.
- Brush a small amount of glue on tree (sketch a). Lay several pieces of tissue onto glue. (Make sure slits in trees are not covered with tissue.)
- Repeat process until trees are covered with tissue (sketch b). Brush over tissue paper with a layer of glue.
- With teacher's help, slide one tree piece into the slit of other tree piece and stand tree up (sketch c).

Simplification Idea: Younger children may crumple tissue and then press onto glue on tree.

Bible Bits: How does your tree remind you of our Bible story? When you go home, you can use your tree to tell your (mom, dad, friend) our story about Zacchaeus.

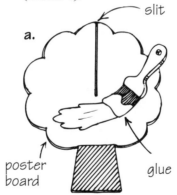

a. slit / poster board / glue

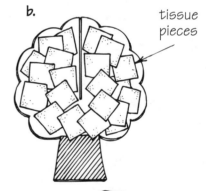

b. tissue pieces

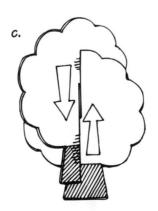

c.

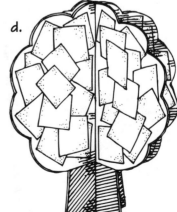

d.

slit 1

slit 2

ZACCHAEUS PUPPET THEATER

(20-25 MINUTES)

Materials
- Jesus and Zacchaeus Puppet Patterns
- nature stickers
- brown paper bags
- resealable plastic sandwich bags

For every two children—
- sheet of green poster board

For each child—
- two tongue depressors

Standard Supplies
- photocopier
- white card stock
- crayons
- glue
- transparent tape
- scissors
- ruler

Preparation: Cut poster board in half widthwise—one half for each child. Cut the top of each half to look like trees (sketch a). Fold each side of board to meet in the middle. Cut out a 2-inch (5-cm) circle in center section. Photocopy Jesus and Zacchaeus Puppet Patterns onto card stock—one set for each child. Cut out or tear tree trunk shapes from brown paper bags—three for each child.

Instruct each child in the following procedures:
- Glue tree trunks to the poster-board puppet theater (sketch a).
- Place nature stickers on the trees and the ground of the theater scene.
- Color Jesus and Zacchaeus. Cut out. (Younger children may need teacher's help.)
- Glue Jesus and Zacchaeus to tongue depressors to make puppets (sketch b).
- Tape sides of plastic bag to back of poster board theater (sketch c). Keep puppets in bag, so they won't get lost.
- Tell your friends or family the story of Zacchaeus by using your puppet theater!

Enrichment Idea: Children may draw people in the crowd near the bottom of the poster board.

Bible Bits: **Zacchaeus was a short man. He climbed up in a tree so that he could see Jesus. What did Jesus say to Zacchaeus when He saw him in the tree?** ("Zacchaeus, I want to go to your house today.") **Zacchaeus was happy that Jesus wanted to be his friend. Jesus is your friend, too. Jesus cares about you very much.**

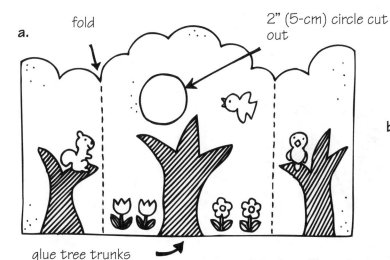

a. fold

2" (5-cm) circle cut out

glue tree trunks

b.

glue tongue depressor to back of puppet

Jesus and Zacchaeus Puppet Patterns

c.

tape

CLAY COINS
(10-15 MINUTES)

Materials
- air-drying clay
- pennies
- nickels
- quarters
- embossed buttons
- waxed paper
- permanent felt pen

Preparation: Tear waxed paper into squares for children to work on—one for each child. Letter child's name on waxed paper square with permanent felt pen. Give each child a piece of clay.

Instruct each child in the following procedures:
- Make several small balls of clay.
- Flatten each ball with your fingers (sketch a).
- Press coin or button onto top of clay circles to make a design (sketch b).
- Let your clay coins dry on waxed paper overnight until hard.

Enrichment Idea: Teacher paints coins with gold or silver spray paint after clay has dried.

Bible Bits: Jesus told a story about a master who asked his servants to help take care of his money while he was gone. Two of the servants used the money to make even more money for their master. They were good helpers! The master was very happy with them and gave them a reward. But the third servant didn't help his master at all. He buried his money in the ground. The master was very unhappy with the lazy servant. Jesus wants us to be good helpers. How can you help at home?

a.

b.

HOSANNA STREAMERS
(10-15 MINUTES)

Materials
- crepe-paper streamers in various bright colors
- string
- assorted stickers

For each child—
- one large plastic or wooden thread spool

Standard Supplies
- transparent tape
- scissors
- measuring stick

Preparation: Remove labels from spools. Cut crepe paper into 1-yard (.9-m) lengths—three different colors for each child. Cut string into 18-inch (45-cm) lengths—one for each child.

Instruct each child in the following procedures:
- Fold one end of streamer into a point (sketch a). Repeat for other two streamers.
- Tape points of streamers onto spool (sketch b).
- Decorate streamers with stickers.
- Thread string through center of spool. With teacher's help, tie a knot to secure string (sketch b).
- Hold spool by string, wave in the air and shout "Hosanna!"
- Wind streamers around spool when not in use.

Enrichment Idea: Instead of holding spool by string, make a long handle by inserting and gluing a dowel into center of spool (sketch c).

Bible Bits: **When Jesus came into town, the people were happy to see Him. What did they shout?** (Hosanna! Hosanna!) **They were glad Jesus had come. Today we're glad Jesus came, too. Jesus came because He loves each one of us.**

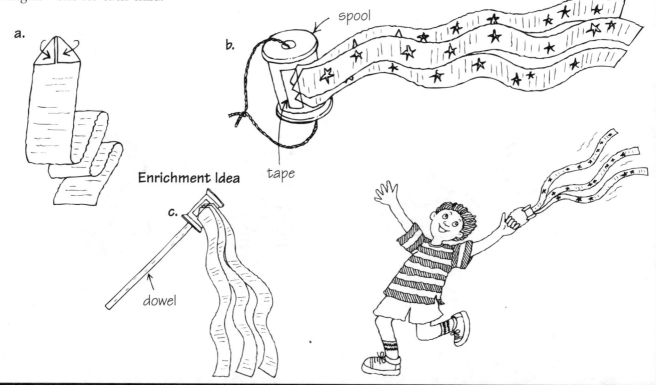

a.

spool

b.

tape

Enrichment Idea

c.

dowel

NEW LIFE BUTTERFLY
(20-25 MINUTES)

Materials
- Butterfly Wings Pattern
- Fun Foam or felt in various colors
- acrylic jewels
- black chenille wire
- permanent felt pen

For each child—
- one plastic spoon

Standard Supplies
- pen
- craft glue
- scissors
- ruler

Preparation: With permanent pen, trace Butterfly Wings Pattern onto Fun Foam or felt and cut out—one for each child. With felt pen, letter "Jesus Is Alive" on each spoon handle. Cut chenille wires in half—one half for each child. Cut Fun Foam or felt scraps into 1-inch (2.5-cm) -sized triangles, circles and squares.

Instruct each child in the following procedures:
- With felt pen, draw a face on indentation of spoon.
- Glue Fun Foam wings to the back of spoon (see sketch).
- Bend chenille wire in half and curl each end for antennae. Glue to back of butterfly head.
- Glue jewels and Fun Foam or felt shapes on the wings to decorate.
- When glue has dried, hold on to the spoon handle and wave back and forth to make your butterfly fly!

Bible Bits: **A butterfly begins its life as a caterpillar. One day the caterpillar spins a cocoon and no one sees it for a long time. When it finally comes out of the cocoon, what is different about it?** (It has pretty wings. It's a butterfly.) **The caterpillar starts a new life as a butterfly. Your butterfly says on it "Jesus Is Alive!" Jesus loves you so much that He died and came back to life. Someday you can have a new life with Him in heaven!**

glue chenille wire to back

JESUS IS ALIVE!

glue wings to back of spoon

BUTTERFLY WINGS PATTERN

CLOTHESPIN ANGEL

(10-15 MINUTES)

Materials

- white spray paint
- white chenille wire
- white or pastel-colored tulle (available at fabric stores)
- cotton balls
- fine-tip permanent felt pen

For each child—

- one wooden clothespin (non-spring-type)

Standard Supplies

- glue
- scissors
- ruler
- newspaper

Preparation: Lay clothespins on newspaper in a well-ventilated area and spray with white spray paint. Allow to dry. Then turn over to paint the opposite side and allow to dry. Cut tulle into 3×6-inch (7.5×15-cm) rectangles—one for each child. Cut chenille wires in half—one half for each child.

Instruct each child in the following procedures:

- Pinch the tulle together in the center to make wings.
- Hold together while teacher helps twist chenille wire around the center of tulle (sketch a).
- Place wings against back of clothespin.
- Wrap chenille wire around the neck of the clothespin twice, leaving ends in front to form arms (sketch b).
- Fold chenille wire ends under to form hands.
- Pull cotton ball apart to flatten and then glue onto top of clothespin for hair.
- Use felt pen to draw face.

Bible Bits: **What good news did the angels tell the women when they went to the tomb?** (Jesus is alive!) **The women ran to tell their friends the happy news. We can be happy that Jesus came back to life, too. Now He can be our friend forever.**

cotton ball

b.

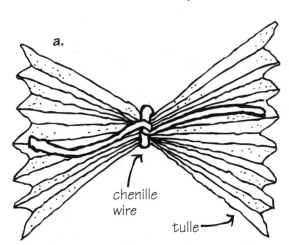

a.

chenille wire

tulle

"HE IS RISEN" SHADOWBOX
(30-35 MINUTES)

Materials
- Angel Picture
- tempera paint in gray, brown and green
- course sand or bird grit
- yarn
- paper clips
- mixing bowl
- measuring cups and spoons
- mixing spoon

For each child—
- two sturdy, large paper plates
- one paper fastener

Standard Supplies
- photocopier
- copier paper
- lightweight cardboard
- crayons
- glue
- paintbrushes
- scissors
- hole punch
- shallow containers
- ruler
- newspaper

Preparation: Cut out center of plate slightly smaller than the size of Angel Picture (sketch a)—one plate for each child. Cut cardboard into circles or stone shapes the same size as Angel Picture—

one for each child. With hole punch, punch one hole close to the edge of each cardboard shape. Photocopy Angel Picture onto paper—one for each child. Cut yarn into 6-inch (15-cm) lengths—one for each child. Make textured paint by mixing in bowl 2 cups of gray paint, ½ cup of grit or sand and 4 tablespoons of white glue. Cover work area with newspaper. Pour textured paint into shallow containers. Pour brown and green paint into shallow containers.

Instruct each child in the following procedures:
- Paint the underside of cut plate brown for a cave and green for grass (sketch b).
- Paint one side of cardboard circle with gray textured paint. Set aside to dry.
- Use crayons to color Angel Picture.
- Cut out picture and glue to front center of uncut plate.
- Once painted paper plate is dry, with teacher's help, punch two holes in the cut-out paper plate as indicated in sketch c. Punch a hole at the top of uncut plate.

- Line up the holes at the top of paper plates and glue the rims of plates together. The Angel Picture will show through the cut-out paper plate. Have teacher paper clip edges until glue has dried (sketch c).
- With teacher's help, attach the painted "stone" to the top paper plate with a paper fastener (sketch d).
- Thread yarn through hole at top of plates and tie for a hanger.
- Cover the opening with the stone; then roll it away to see the angel tell the happy news that Jesus is risen!

Enrichment Ideas: Children may glue dried flowers and greenery onto grass portion of paper plate.

Bible Bits: **What did the angel tell Jesus' friends when they saw the empty tomb?** (Jesus is alive. He is risen.) **Jesus' friends were very happy. We can be happy that Jesus is alive, too. We can pray to Jesus anytime. We can talk to Him when we are afraid, sad or happy. Jesus loves and cares for us.**

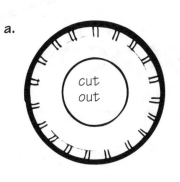

a.

cut
out

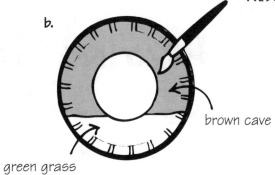

b.

brown cave

green grass

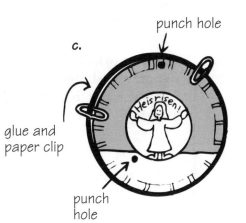

punch hole

c.

glue and
paper clip

He is risen!

punch
hole

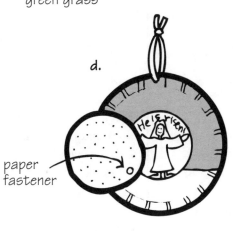

d.

paper
fastener

He is risen!

ANGEL PICTURE

He is risen!

PRAYING HANDS BOOK

(10-15 MINUTES)

Materials

◆ instant camera and film

Standard Supplies

◆ 8½×11-inch (21.5×27.5-cm) sheets of card stock
◆ felt pen
◆ crayons
◆ glue
◆ scissors
◆ ruler

Preparation: Cut card stock in half—one half for each child. Then fold each half to make books. Use instant camera to take a picture of each child.

Instruct each child in the following procedures:

◆ Open book and lay the inside of book down flat. Place both hands flat on book cover with both thumbs touching fold line in center.
◆ Teacher uses crayon to trace around both hands.
◆ Color each hand (sketch a).
◆ On the inside of book, glue your picture on one page (sketch b).
◆ Teacher letters the child's prayer or comment on prayer on the opposite page in book.

Simplification Idea: Children use crayons to draw pictures of themselves in book instead of gluing photos.

Bible Bits: When are times that you pray, (Kristoffer)? What would you like to say to God today?

a.

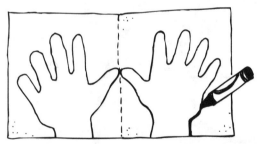

b.

PRAYER PLACE MAT
(15-20 MINUTES)

Materials
- several magazines with various pictures (showing animals, foods, people, nature, etc.)
- poster board in various colors
- clear Con-Tact paper

Standard Supplies
- glue sticks
- scissors
- measuring stick

Preparations: Cut poster board into 9×12-inch (22.5×30-cm) mats—one for each child. On each mat letter at the top, "Dear God, thank You for..." and at the bottom write "Amen." Cut Con-Tact paper into 10×13-inch (25×32.5-cm) rectangles—two for each child. Look through magazines and tear out appropriate pages. (For younger children, cut out individual pictures.)

Instruct each child in the following procedures:
- Cut out magazine pictures of people or things that you are thankful that God has made or given to you.
- Glue cutouts onto poster-board mat.
- With teacher's help, peel adhesive backing from Con-Tact paper and place on front of place mat, smoothing out any wrinkles. Then peel adhesive backing from second piece of Con-Tact paper and repeat process on back of place mat.
- With teacher's help, cut edges of Con-Tact paper as close as possible to edges of place mats.

Bible Bits: You can use your Prayer Place Mat to help you remember to thank God when you pray. (Kelly), your place mat says, "Dear God, thank you for... Point to pictures and name each out loud. **Amen!**"

cover both sides with Con-Tact paper

Dear God, thank You for...

Amen.

PRAYING HANDS DESIGN
(10-15 MINUTES)

Materials
- liquid tempera paint
- old sponges
- yarn
- small stickers

Standard Supplies
- colored card stock
- pencils
- felt pens
- transparent tape
- scissors
- hole punch
- ruler
- shallow containers
- newspaper

Preparation: Cut sponges into 2-inch (5-cm) pieces. Cover work area with newspaper. Pour tempera paint into shallow containers.

Instruct each child in the following procedures:
- Place one hand palm down, with fingers together, on one sheet of card stock. Leave at least ½-inch (1.25-cm) margins at top, bottom and outside edges.
- Teacher traces around hand, cuts out and discards hand print (sketch a).
- Tape the hand pattern stencil over another sheet of card stock (sketch b).
- Dip sponge piece into paint and then press onto the hand cutout. Cover the entire hand design.

- Allow to dry and then remove stencil.
- Decorate the edges of card stock by applying stickers.
- Teacher letters the child's prayer or comment on prayer next to hand (sketch c).
- Punch a hole in the top corners. With teacher's help, thread yarn through holes and tie to make hanger.

Bible Bits: **When we pray, we are talking to God. When are times that you pray? What would you like to talk to God about right now?**

a.

cut out

discard

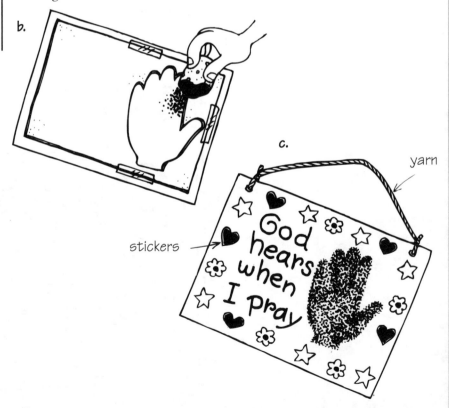

b.

c.

yarn

stickers

God hears when I pray

SUNSHINE MOBILE
(15-20 MINUTES)

Materials
- several magazines with various pictures
- large yellow paper plates
- yarn
- hammer
- nail
- wood scrap
- black permanent felt pen

For each child—
- four frozen-juice can lids (any size)

Standard Supplies
- orange and yellow construction paper
- glue
- scissors
- hole punch
- ruler

Preparation: Cut paper plates in half—one half for each child. Cut yarn into 12-inch (30-cm) lengths—five for each child. Cut construction paper into 2-inch (5-cm) squares; then cut in half to make triangles. Place juice can lids on wood scrap surface. Use hammer and nail to make a hole at top of each lid (sketch a). Tie yarn through hole in each lid. Look through magazines and tear out pages with small pictures of items that a child might be thankful for. With black pen, letter "Thank You, God, for..." along edge of paper plate (sketch b).

Instruct each child in the following procedures:
- With teacher's help, punch four evenly spaced holes along bottom edge of plate and one on top (sketch b).
- Glue paper triangles around curved edge of paper plate.
- Cut out magazine pictures of people, animals or things for which you are thankful.
- Glue pictures onto both sides of juice can lids.
- With teacher's help, tie lids to plate (sketch b). Trim yarn ends if needed.
- To make hanger, tie yarn through hole on top.

Simplification Ideas: Eliminate paper triangles. For younger children, teacher cuts out small pictures from magazines.

Bible Bits: What are you thankful for, (Andre)? God takes care of you. He helps you have what you need to grow up healthy and strong. We can tell God we are glad that He takes care of us. We can thank Him for our (family, pets, food, etc.), too.

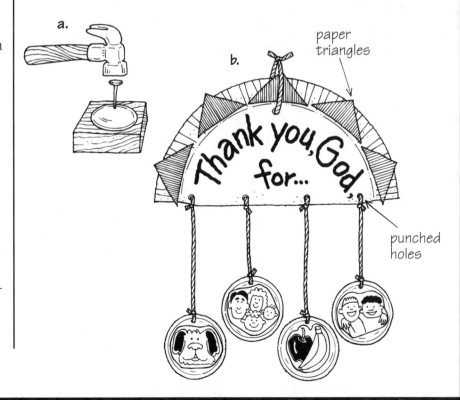

a.

b.

paper triangles

punched holes

Thank you, God, for...

FLIP-FLOP FACE
(20-25 MINUTES)

Materials
◆ Fun Foam or construction paper in various colors
◆ yarn

For each child—
◆ two small white paper plates
◆ one tongue depressor

Standard Supplies
◆ glue
◆ scissors

Preparation: From Fun Foam or construction paper, cut out shapes for eyebrows, eyes, nose and mouth for faces (see sketches a and b). Cut lengths of yarn for hair.

Instruct each child in the following procedures:
◆ Glue happy-face features to back side of one paper plate. Glue on yarn for hair (sketch a).
◆ Glue angry-face features to back side of second paper plate. Glue on yarn for hair (sketch b).
◆ Glue tongue depressor to front edge of one plate (sketch c).
◆ Glue front rims of plates together.
◆ Allow glue to dry.

Simplification Idea: Children draw faces on paper plates instead of gluing on shapes.

Bible Bits: **(Mariah), how do you feel when someone is angry with you? How do you feel when you make a mistake and someone shows you love instead of anger? When you feel angry, you can ask God to help you forgive and show love instead of hurting others.**

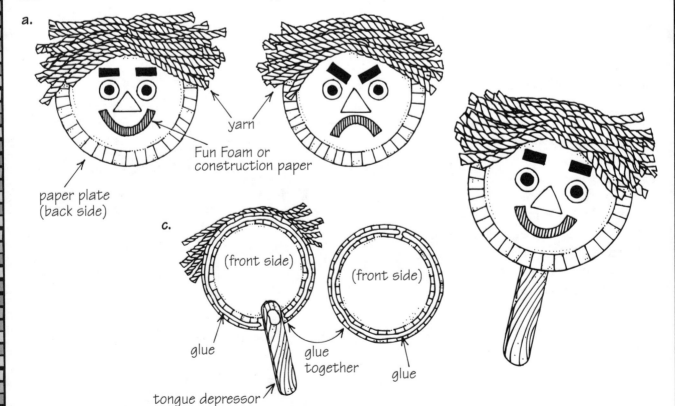

a.

b.

yarn

Fun Foam or
construction paper

paper plate
(back side)

c.

(front side)

(front side)

glue

glue
together

glue

tongue depressor

LOVE MEDALLION
(10-15 MINUTES)

Materials
◆ yarn
◆ macaroni
◆ gold spray paint
◆ small-size margarine lid

Standard Supplies
◆ poster board
◆ colored felt pens
◆ pencil
◆ glue
◆ hole punch
◆ scissors
◆ measuring stick
◆ newspaper

Preparation: Trace around margarine lid to make circles on poster board—one circle for each child. Cut out circles. With felt pens, letter "Love" on each circle. Punch hole at top of circle. Cut a 24-inch (60-cm) length of yarn for each child. Place macaroni on newspaper in a well-ventilated area and spray with paint.

Instruct each child in the following procedures:
◆ Glue macaroni around edge of circle medallion.
◆ With teacher's help, push end of yarn through hole and tie for necklace.

Enrichment Idea: Older children may copy the letters onto poster board themselves.

Bible Bits: God shows love to you by giving you people who love and take care of you. How do people show love to you? What are some ways you can show love to others? How can we show love to God?

glue

HEART MAGNET
(10-15 MINUTES)

Materials
♦ Heart Pattern
♦ ½-inch (1.25-cm) pom-poms in various colors
♦ self-adhesive magnetic strips

For each child—
♦ small picture or sticker of Jesus

Standard Supplies
♦ poster board
♦ pencil
♦ glue
♦ scissors
♦ ruler

Preparation: Trace Heart Pattern onto poster board—one for each child. Cut out heart shapes. Cut self-adhesive magnetic strips into 1-inch (2.5-cm) pieces.

Instruct each child in the following procedures:
♦ Glue picture or attach sticker of Jesus in center of poster-board heart.
♦ Turn heart over and attach a self-adhesive magnetic strip to the back of the heart shape (sketch a).
♦ Turn heart faceup again. Squeeze a thin line of glue around outside edge of heart.
♦ Glue pom-poms around heart (sketch b).

Bible Bits: When you look at your Heart Magnet, you can remember how much Jesus loves you. What is one thing Jesus did to show us how much He loves us?

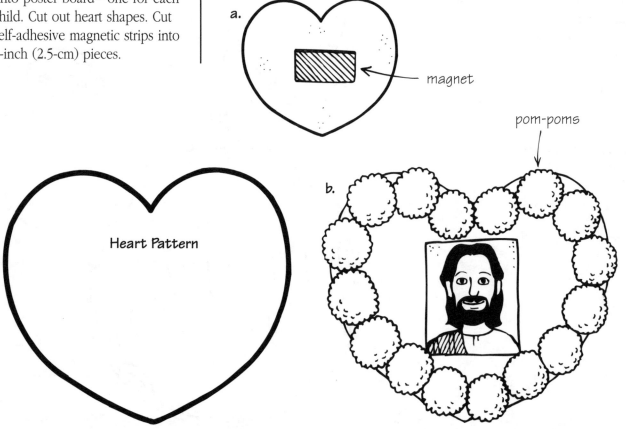

a.

magnet

Heart Pattern

b.

pom-poms

"DO GOOD" PIE
(20-25 MINUTES)

Materials
- cinnamon-spice scented pot-pourri
- coffee scoops or small-sized measuring cups
- toothpicks

For each child—
- one 4½-inch (11.25-cm) aluminum pie pan

Standard Supplies
- tan construction paper
- orange and brown felt pens or crayons
- pencils
- hot-glue gun and glue sticks
- scissors
- ruler
- shallow containers

Preparation: Cut construction paper into 5-inch (12.5-cm) squares—one for each child. Trace around a pie pan to make a circle on each tan square. In the center of each circle, use a brown felt pen to write the words "Do Good." Place potpourri in shallow containers. Plug in glue gun out of reach of children.

Instruct each child in the following procedures:
- Cut out the construction-paper circle.
- With orange or brown felt pens or crayons, draw short lines around the edge of circle to look like a baked crust (sketch a).
- Use scoop or measuring cup to fill your pie pan with potpourri.
- Teacher squeezes hot glue on edge of pie pan and glues tan circle on top for piecrust (sketch b). Allow glue to cool.
- Use a toothpick to punch holes in the crust, on the lines of the words "Do Good" (sketch c).
- Smell your pretend pie! Mmmmmm...

Enrichment Idea: Have children mix potpourri together using cinnamon sticks, wood shavings, scented oils, lavender, dried flowers, etc.

Bible Bits: (Kristen), what is your favorite kind of pie? (Child responds.) **You can't eat your potpourri pie. It's just pretend. But it smells wonderful! You may set it in your room to make your room smell good or you may give your pie to someone you love. What will you do with your pie?**

a.
draw "crust" lines

DO GOOD

b.
DO GOOD
potpourri
glue pie pan edge

c.
punch holes with toothpick
DO GOOD

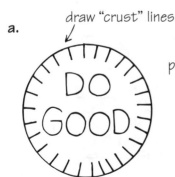

"BUILD THE CASTLE" PICTURE

(15—20 MINUTES)

Materials
- Castle Picture
- square-shaped cereal (such as Chex)
- 1-inch (2.5-cm) wide ribbon

For each child—
- two craft sticks

Standard Supplies
- photocopier
- white card stock
- colored felt pens
- glue
- fabric scissors
- all-purpose scissors
- ruler
- shallow containers

Preparation: Photocopy Castle Picture onto card stock—one for each child. Use all-purpose scissors to cut craft sticks in half—four halves for each child. Use fabric scissors to cut ribbon into 1½-inch (3.75-cm) pieces—two for each child. Cut half the ribbon pieces in half diagonally to make pennants—two pennants for each child. Cut the remaining ribbon pieces into banner shapes—one for each child (sketch a). Pour cereal into shallow containers. Pour glue into other shallow containers.

Instruct each child in the following procedures:
- Color the banner above the door with a light-colored felt pen.
- Glue craft sticks onto door of castle.
- Dip pieces of cereal into glue, one at a time, and stick onto castle bricks (sketch b).
- Glue ribbon pieces to flag poles to make pennants and banner (sketch b). Allow glue to dry.

Enrichment Idea: Fold back the sides of poster board to make castle stand.

Bible Bits: **The banner above your castle door says,** *God made us to do good*. **(Laurin), what can you do to help your (mom/friend/teacher)?** (Child responds.) **When you (feed the cat), you are doing good. God wants us to do good things!**

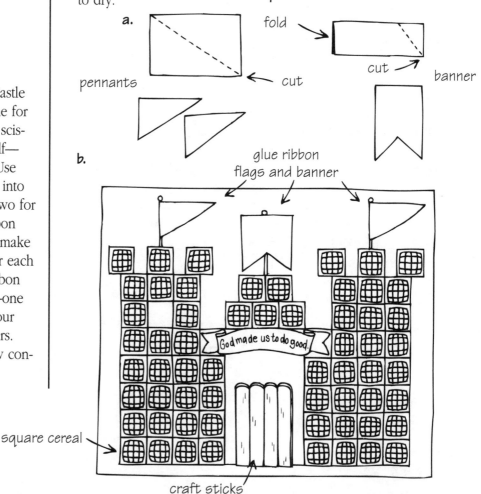

a.

pennants   fold   cut   cut   banner

b.

glue ribbon flags and banner

God made us to do good.

square cereal

craft sticks

CASTLE PICTURE

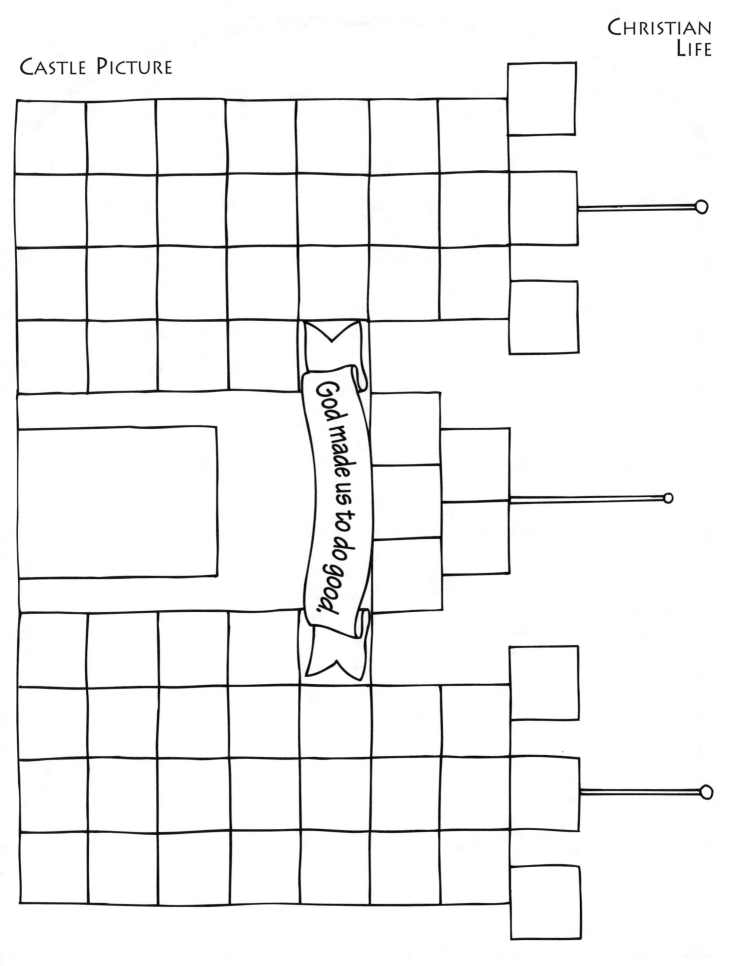

God made us to do good.

The Big Book of Bible Crafts

CHURCH WINDOW FRAME
(15–20 MINUTES)

Materials
- Window Frame Patterns
- mat board or poster board
- heavy cardboard
- metallic gold spray paint
- pasta in various shapes
- rubbing alcohol
- food coloring in three different colors
- cotton swabs

Standard Supplies
- pencil
- white glue
- sharp scissors or craft knife
- paintbrushes
- ruler
- shallow containers
- newspaper

Preparation: Trace Frame Front Pattern onto mat board or poster board—one for each child. Trace Frame Back Pattern and Stand Pattern onto cardboard—one of each for each child. Cut out all frame pieces with scissors or craft knife. Use sharp scissors or craft knife to score a line ½ inch (1.25 cm) from one end of each stand piece (sketch a). Lay frame fronts and some of the pasta pieces on newspaper in a well-ventilated area and spray with gold paint.

Dye the remaining pasta three bright colors as follows: Pour some alcohol into shallow containers—one container for each color. Add several drops of food coloring. Put pasta into alcohol

just long enough for color to be absorbed. Spread pasta on newspaper to dry.

Pour glue into shallow containers. Put colored pasta into separate shallow containers.

Instruct each child in the following procedures:
- Use swab to spread glue along the side and bottom edges of frame back (sketch b).
- Press unpainted side of frame front onto glued frame back.
- Spread a thick coat of glue on the front of gold frame.
- Place gold and colored pasta on the glue to decorate frame.
- With teacher's help, spread glue on scored section of stand and glue onto frame back with bottom edges even (sketch c). Let dry.

Enrichment Idea: One or two days before project, teacher photographs and develops 3×5-inch (7.5×12.5-cm) individual vertical pictures of children. Children insert photo in completed frame.

Bible Bits: (Karina), you may put a picture of someone you love in your Church Window Frame. Who is someone you love? (Child responds.) **Who is someone who loves you?** (Child responds.) **God loves you, too. Our Bible says,** *God loved us and sent Jesus* **(see 1 John 4:10). Jesus came to show His love for us and to teach us how to love each other.**

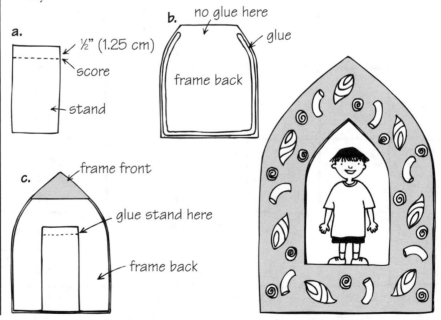

a.
½" (1.25 cm)
score
stand

b.
no glue here
glue
frame back

c.
frame front
glue stand here
frame back

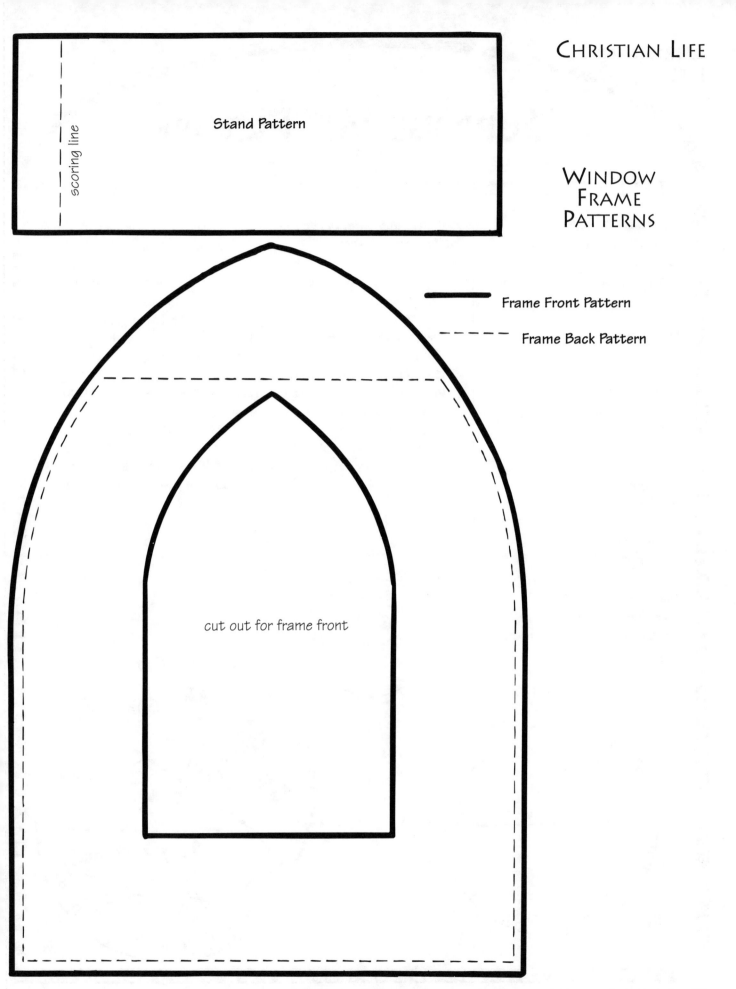

CHRISTIAN LIFE

scoring line

Stand Pattern

WINDOW
FRAME
PATTERNS

Frame Front Pattern

Frame Back Pattern

cut out for frame front

"SURPRISE ME" PICTURE
(10-15 MINUTES)

Materials
- pink and brown construction paper
- a variety of rubber stamps and ink pads, or stickers in various designs

For each child—
- one white paper plate
- one paper fastener

Standard Supplies
- crayons
- glue sticks
- scissors
- hole punch
- ruler

Preparation: For each child—cut paper plate in half (sketch a). On the back side of the top half of plate, letter "God loves." On the back side of the bottom half, letter the child's name. (Older children may wish to write their own names.) Cut 5-inch (12.5-cm) circles from pink and brown construction paper.

Instruct each child in the following procedures:
- With crayons, draw your face on a construction-paper circle (sketch b). (Younger children may need to look at a simple "happy face" sample.)
- Rub glue stick on the front lower edge of face and glue to the straight edge of the paper plate that has your name on it (sketch c).
- Decorate the plate halves by stamping with rubber stamp or applying stickers.

- Place paper plate halves facing each other, with lettered side up.
- With teacher's help, punch a hole in the left edge of each half; then fasten paper plate halves together with a paper fastener (sketch c).

Bible Bits: **Let's see who God loves!** Have children open pictures to reveal the circle they drew of themselves. **Oh, look! God loves (Aimee)! I'm glad that God loves each one of us!**

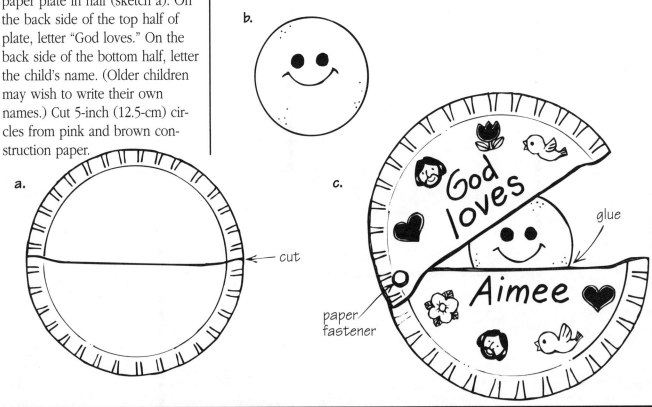

b.

a. ← cut

c.

God loves

Aimee

glue

paper fastener

CRAFTS FOR ELEMENTARY CHILDREN

Children in the first few years of elementary school delight in completing craft projects. They have a handle on most of the basic skills needed, are eager to participate, and their taste in art hasn't yet surpassed their ability to produce. In other words, they generally like the things they make.

Trying to plan craft projects for older elementary children, however, can present a challenge. Although older children possess well-developed skills to complete projects, they also have well-developed preferences about what they want to do. A project that challenges their abilities may be scorned because it somehow doesn't appeal to these young sophisticates. Yet another project that seems too juvenile to the adult will click with the kids. Being flexible and keeping your sense of humor can certainly help!

We think that throughout this section you will find a variety of projects to satisfy the tastes and abilities of younger *and* older elementary children.

CREATION WINDOW
(25-30 MINUTES)

Materials
♦ discarded magazines

For each child—
♦ paper plate
♦ paper fastener

Standard Supplies
♦ construction paper
♦ felt pens
♦ glue
♦ scissors
♦ ruler

Preparation: Cut 8-inch (20-cm) circles from construction paper—one for each child. Cut out a 2-inch (5-cm) square in each paper plate (sketch a).

Instruct each child in the following procedures:
♦ With felt pen, letter "God Created" on plates.
♦ Find small magazine pictures that illustrate what God created on each of the six days of creation (light, sky, earth and plants, moon and stars, birds and fish, animals and man) and cut them out.
♦ Glue the pictures evenly around the outside of construction-paper circle (sketch b).
♦ Attach paper plate to the circle by pushing paper fastener through the center of both (sketch c).
♦ Turn wheel to see the days of creation through the window.

Bible Bits: **What is the most unusual thing you have seen that God has created? What do you think is the most beautiful thing? God made our world so interesting. Some people may like the desert, while other people like the forests. Some people think bugs are great, while other people love tropical fish. God created our world so that everyone can enjoy it.**

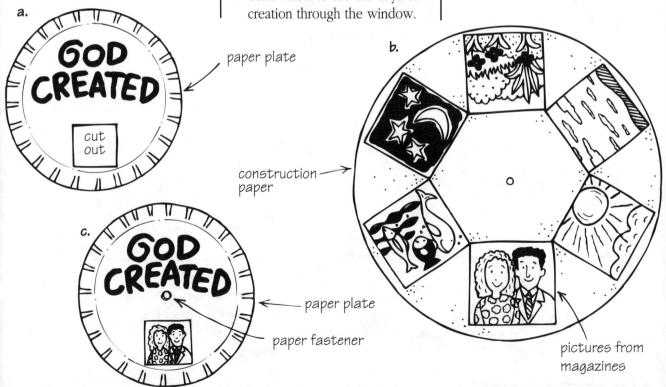

"GOD'S WORLD" PAPERWEIGHT
(20-25 MINUTES)

Materials
- felt
- small nature items (shells, dried flowers, pinecones, rocks, etc.)
- poster board

For each child—
- one 6-oz. clear glass or clear plastic custard cup

Standard Supplies
- paper
- felt pen
- craft glue
- scissors
- ruler

Preparation: Cut poster board and felt into 5-inch (12.5-cm) squares—one of each for each child.

Instruct each child in the following procedures:
- Turn custard cup upside down on poster-board square and trace around cup with felt pen. Cut out.
- Repeat procedure with felt and felt pen (sketch a).
- Glue felt circle to poster-board circle.
- Cut a small strip of paper. With felt pen, on the strip write "God made the world."
- Glue strip to the bottom portion of felt circle (sketch b).
- Glue shells, dried flowers or other nature items onto center of felt circle.
- Squeeze a line of glue around the outer edge of the felt circle and press inverted custard cup onto glue.
- Set aside to dry.

Bible Bits: What are some things you might see if you were hiking in the woods? walking on the beach? camping in the desert? We can be thankful that God has made so many wonderful things for us to enjoy.

a.

felt

poster board

b.

God made the world

FLUTTER BUTTERFLY
(20-25 MINUTES)

Materials
- Flutter Butterfly Pattern
- thin tempera paints in squeeze bottles

For each child—
- one tongue depressor
- half of a black chenille wire
- one spring-type clothespin
- one drinking straw

Standard Supplies
- photocopier
- white paper
- black wide-tip felt pens
- glue
- scissors
- newspaper

Preparation: Photocopy Flutter Butterfly Pattern onto paper—one for each child. Cut chenille wires in half. Cover work area with newspaper.

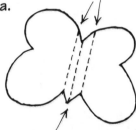

a.

fold

center fold

b.

Instruct each child in the following procedures:
- Cut out paper butterfly.
- Fold butterfly on the center fold line; then fold back on outer fold lines (sketch a). Lay paper with center fold pointing down.
- Squeeze small drops of paint onto one butterfly wing.
- With straw, gently blow paint drops to make designs.
- Press wings together to print painted wing on unpainted wing. Open wings and allow to dry.
- Color both sides of tongue depressor with felt pen.
- Fold chenille wire around one end of tongue depressor. Twist ends of wire together to secure around tongue depressor. Spread apart and bend ends to make antennae (sketch b).

- Glue tongue depressor inside fold of wings.
- Clip clothespin to underside of butterfly.
- Hold clothespin and move your hand up and down to make your butterfly flutter.

Bible Bits: **God created butterflies in many different colors and patterns. He created us with many different colors of eyes, hair and skin, too. God loves us and made us all special!**

FLUTTER BUTTERFLY PATTERN

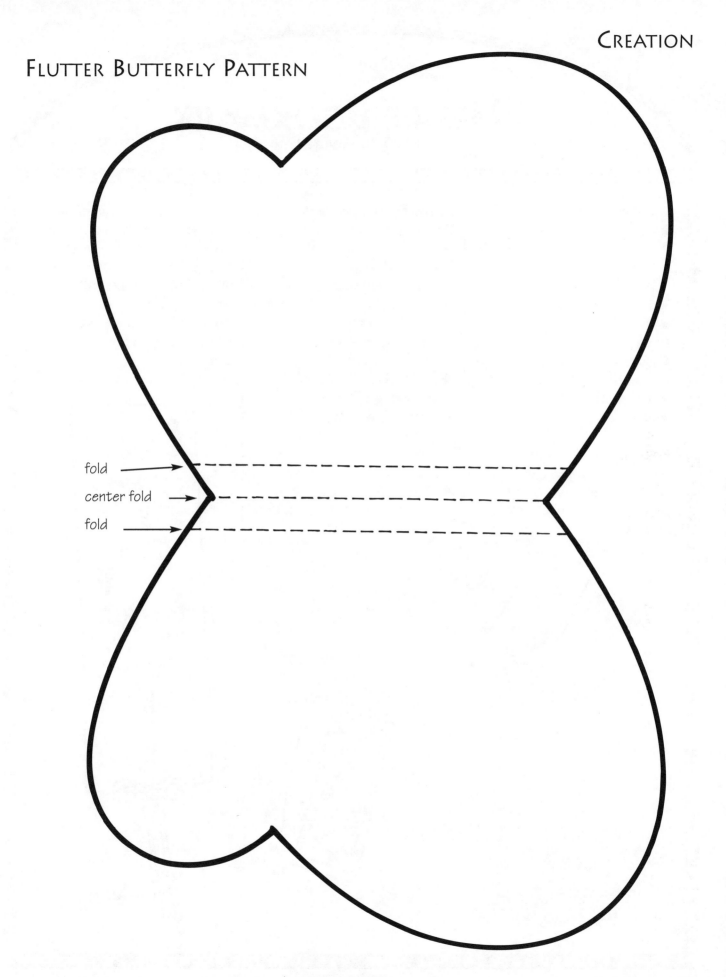

fold →

center fold →

fold →

NATURE BOOKMARK
(15-20 MINUTES)

Materials
- clear Con-Tact paper
- small dried flowers and leaves
- yarn

Standard Supplies
- colored card stock
- colored fine-tip felt pens
- glue
- scissors
- hole punch
- ruler

Preparation: Cut card stock and clear Con-Tact paper into 2×6-inch (5×15-cm) strips—one for each child. Cut yarn into 6-inch (15-cm) lengths.

Instruct each child in the following procedures:
- Letter "God made all things" on card-stock strip.
- Decorate bookmark by gluing on dried flowers and leaves (sketch a). Use a very small amount of glue and allow to dry for a few minutes.
- Peel backing off Con-Tact paper strip and carefully cover bookmark (sketch b).
- Use a hole punch to make a hole in one end of the bookmark.
- Thread yarn through hole, tie in a knot and then tie a bow. Trim yarn ends to make even.

Bible Bits: **What is the most important book you can read?** (The Bible.) **You can use your bookmark in your Bible. The Bible tells us about God's creation of the world. God made all things. God made you. That's why God loves you so much.**

Con-Tact strip

ADAM'S ANIMAL MAGNETS
(15-20 MINUTES)

Materials
- animal crackers
- acrylic paint in various colors
- clear nail polish
- narrow magnet strips

Standard Supplies
- craft glue
- scissors
- paintbrushes
- shallow containers
- ruler
- newspaper

Preparation: Cut magnet strips into ½-inch (1.25-cm) lengths—two for each child. Cover work area with newspaper. Pour paint into shallow containers.

Instruct each child in the following procedures:
- Choose two unbroken crackers. (*Note:* Have extra crackers available, as they break easily.)
- Paint fronts of crackers and allow to dry.
- In well-ventilated area, brush clear nail polish on fronts and backs of crackers. Let dry.
- Glue magnet piece onto back of each cracker (sketch a). Allow glue to dry.

Simplification Ideas: Omit painting and just use clear nail polish. Or use clear acrylic spray instead of nail polish.

Enrichment Ideas: Make a jewelry pin by gluing a piece of poster board onto back of painted cracker. Glue pin back onto poster board (sketch b). Or glue painted cracker onto a barrette clip.

Bible Bits: **On what day of creation did God make the animals?** (Sixth day.) **God created Adam and Eve, too. What important jobs did they have to do?** (Take care of the garden. Name all the animals.) **What would you name some of the animals if you could name them?**

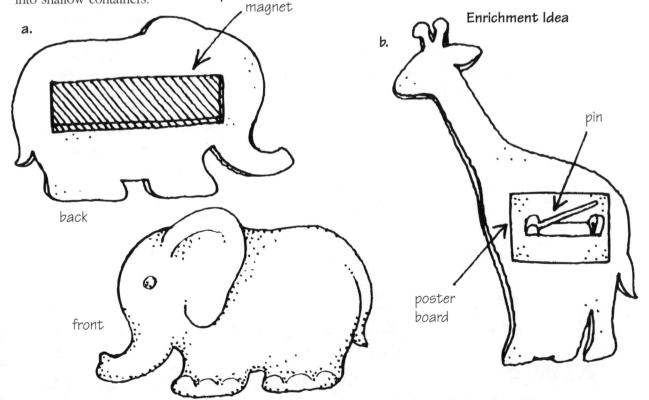

a. magnet

back

front

b. Enrichment Idea

pin

poster board

"GARDEN OF EDEN" FRAME
(25-30 MINUTES)

Materials
- Frame Pattern
- white poster board
- green and blue tissue paper
- tempera paints
- green twisted paper (available at craft stores)
- animal crackers

Standard Supplies
- pencil
- glue
- paintbrushes
- scissors
- ruler
- shallow containers
- water
- newspaper

Preparation: Cut tissue paper into 2-inch (5-cm) wide strips. Trace Frame Pattern onto poster board to make one frame and one frame back for each child. Cut out frame pieces. Cut twisted paper into 12-inch (30-cm) lengths—one for each child. Cover work area with newspaper. Pour glue into containers and dilute with a little water. Pour paint into containers.

Instruct each child in the following procedures:
- Choose two or three animal crackers and paint with tempera paint. Set aside to dry.
- Tear tissue-paper strips into small squares. Brush picture frame with glue and cover with tissue paper, overlapping squares. Use only one color of tissue, or make a landscape using green for land and blue for sky (sketch a).
- Brush a layer of glue over tissue, folding tissue onto back of frame and along edges of opening.
- Untwist green twisted paper length.
- Cut off 1 to 2 inches (2.5 to 5 cm) of paper and glue on bottom and along sides of frame as "plants."
- Glue painted animal crackers in and behind "plants" (sketch b).
- Brush animal crackers and paper plants with glue to seal.

- For hanger, glue the ends of the remaining twisted paper length to the frame backing (sketch c).
- Glue the frame back to the decorated frame. Glue only along the bottom edge and sides to allow for picture insertion at top (sketch c).

Bible Bits: It's important to follow instructions when you make your picture frame. What would happen if you didn't follow the instructions? (We wouldn't know how to do the craft.) **God gave Adam and Eve instructions to follow, too. What instructions did God ask Adam and Eve to follow?** (Eat the fruit of every tree in the garden, *except* the tree of the knowledge of good and evil.) **God gives all of us instructions to follow and they are in the Bible. God wants us to obey Him because He loves us and knows what is best for us.**

a.

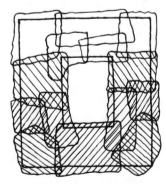

b.

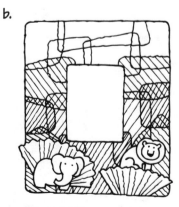

c.

glue

glue around edges

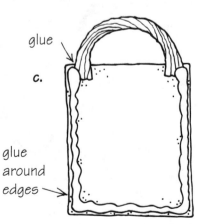

FRAME PATTERN

cut two on solid line

cut out one
for frame front

"GOOD CHOICE" APPLE
(25-30 MINUTES)

Materials
- Apple and Leaf Patterns
- red and green felt
- medium-sized beads

Standard Supplies
- white paper
- lightweight cardboard
- felt pens
- pencils
- glue
- scissors
- ruler

Preparation: Trace Apple Pattern onto lightweight cardboard and cut out—one for each child. Trace Leaf Pattern onto cardboard and cut out—one for every two or three children. Cut remaining cardboard into 1×6-inch (2.5×15-cm) strips—one for each child. Cut paper into 3-inch (7.5-cm) squares—one for each child.

Instruct each child in the following procedures:
- With felt pen, trace cardboard apple onto red felt and cut out.
- Trace Leaf Pattern onto green felt. Cut out.
- Cut a door in the middle of felt apple (sketch a).
- Using felt pen, letter "God says" on door flap.
- To make knob, glue bead onto the right edge of the door.
- Letter "Make good choices" on paper square.
- Glue paper square onto center of cardboard apple (sketch b).
- Glue felt apple to cardboard apple. (Do NOT glue the door. The door opens to reveal lettering behind it.)
- Glue the leaf behind the stem.
- Fold down ends of cardboard strip and then fold cardboard strip in half for stand.
- Glue stand to back of apple (sketch c).

Simplification Idea: Precut apples and leaves from felt.

Bible Bits: Adam and Eve chose to eat the fruit God had told them not to eat. Did they make a good choice? They disobeyed God, but He still loved them. God loves you, too. He wants you to choose to obey Him. In what ways can you obey God? What good choices can you make?

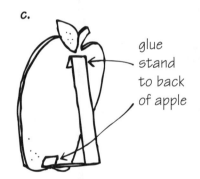

c.

glue stand to back of apple

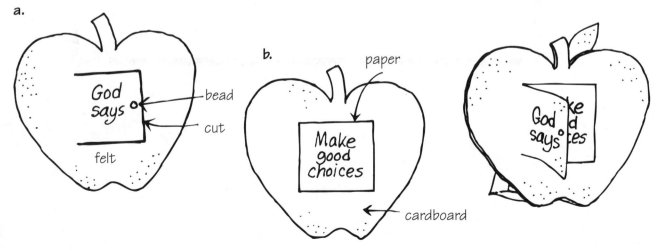

a.

God says

bead

cut

felt

b.

paper

Make good choices

cardboard

God says ke d ces

APPLE AND LEAF PATTERN

cut door here

STAND-UP ARK ANIMALS
(25-30 MINUTES)

Materials
- Animal Patterns
- yarn in various colors including black, brown and yellow
- chenille wire in various colors including black, brown and yellow
- small wiggle eyes

Standard Supplies
- card stock in several bright colors
- felt pens
- pencils
- craft glue
- ruler
- hole punch
- scissors

Preparation: Trace Animal Patterns onto card stock to make several patterns of each. Cut out. Cut remaining card stock into 4×6-inch (10×15-cm) pieces.

Instruct each child in the following procedures:
- Fold a card-stock piece in half and lay an animal body pattern on fold (sketch a). Trace around pattern. Cut out.
- Choosing appropriate patterns, trace and cut out animal heads and other body parts using card-stock pieces.
- Glue wiggle eyes on faces.
- Decorate faces and animal bodies with felt pens, yarn, chenille wire or cut-out card stock.
- For elephant, hippo, lion or cheetah, cut and fold back tabs on body (sketch b).
- Except for lion, glue heads to bodies (sketch c) and allow to dry.

Decorating Animals:
- Zebra: Glue on black chenille wire or yarn for stripes, mane and tail.
- Giraffe: Cut out irregular small card-stock shapes for giraffe markings and glue on. Glue on brown yarn to make short mane and tail. Use brown chenille wire for giraffe antlers.
- Lion: Glue face in the middle of mane. Glue chenille wire or yarn on mane and glue mane to body. Glue on yellow yarn for tail.
- Cheetah: With hole punch, punch out black card-stock spots and glue on. Glue on tail.
- Hippo: Cut out small ears and white tusks. Glue on.
- Elephant: Glue ears on back of head. Cut a strip of card stock and fold accordion style to make trunk. Glue trunk on face.

Enrichment Idea: Children make pairs of animals.

Bible Bits: God kept many different animals safe in the ark. What makes a (zebra) different from every other animal, (Alicia)? God created each animal to be a little different. He created people and made each of us different, too. How are you different from your friends? How are you the same?

ANIMAL PATTERNS

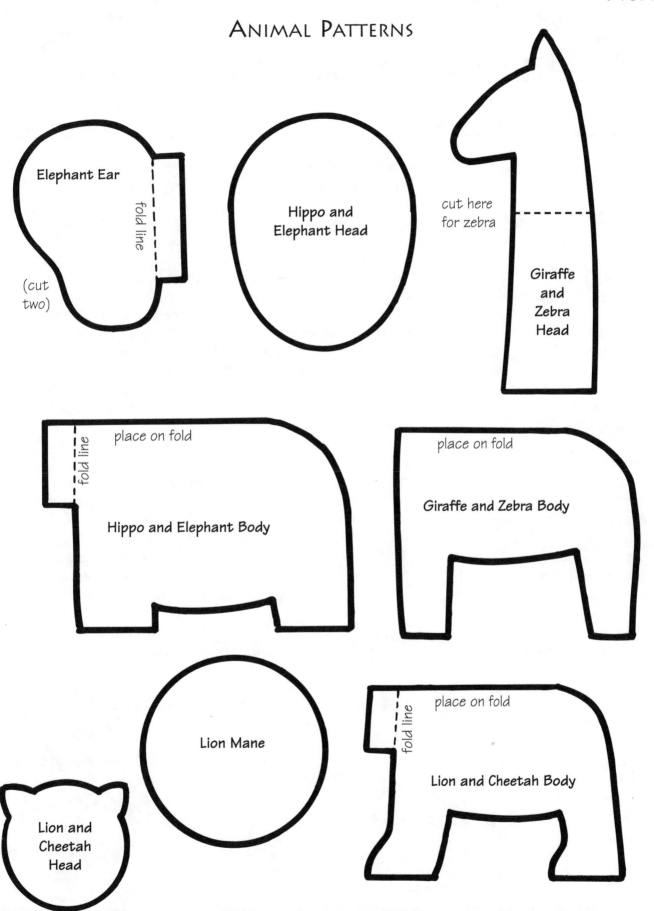

Elephant Ear

fold line

(cut two)

Hippo and Elephant Head

cut here for zebra

Giraffe and Zebra Head

fold line

place on fold

Hippo and Elephant Body

place on fold

Giraffe and Zebra Body

Lion Mane

fold line

place on fold

Lion and Cheetah Body

Lion and Cheetah Head

DRIP-DROP RAINDROP GAME
(30-35 MINUTES)

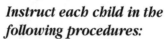

Materials
- Raindrop Pattern
- white poster board
- acrylic paints in rainbow colors
- kitchen sponges
- clear acrylic spray

For each child—
- one gallon-sized milk jug

Standard Supplies
- colored wide-tip felt pens
- pencil
- glue
- paintbrushes
- scissors
- shallow containers
- water
- newspaper

Preparation: Trace Raindrop Pattern onto poster board and cut out 12 raindrops for each child. Cut a large opening in the top of each milk jug, leaving the handle intact (sketch a)—one for each child. Dampen sponges. Cut sponges into cloud shapes. Cover work area with newspaper. Pour paint into containers.

Instruct each child in the following procedures:
- Paint a rainbow on the jug.
- Paint a yellow sun.
- Dip cloud-shaped sponge into blue paint and print several clouds on the jug (sketch b).
- Let jug dry.
- Use felt pens to color six poster-board raindrops one color.
- Glue two raindrops together, colored sides facing out. Repeat to make three double-thick raindrops.
- Color six raindrops using a different color. Glue to make three double-thick raindrops.
- In a well-ventilated area, teacher sprays milk containers with clear acrylic spray. Let dry.

To play with a friend:
- Set jug on the floor. Each player, holding one set of raindrops, stands the same distance from the jug. Taking turns, players try to toss raindrops into the jug.

Enrichment Idea: Children fill small balloons with small amounts of water or sand and tie, making six filled balloons (three each of two different colors). Children use balloons as raindrop game pieces.

Bible Bits: **How many days and nights did it rain while Noah and his family were in the ark?** (Forty days and forty nights.) **What do you like to do on a rainy day? Imagine being on a boat day after day and never being able to go outside to play! God kept Noah, his family and all the animals safe because Noah obeyed God. In what ways can you obey God?**

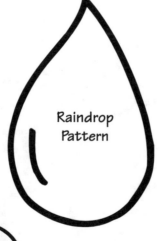

Raindrop Pattern

a.

cut away top

b.

RAINBOW BOOKMARK
(10-15 MINUTES)

Materials
- Cloud Pattern
- grosgrain rainbow ribbon
- white felt
- silver glitter glue

Standard Supplies
- lightweight cardboard
- glue
- scissors
- ruler

Preparation: Trace Cloud Pattern onto lightweight cardboard to make several patterns. Cut out. Cut ribbon into 6-inch (15-cm) lengths—one for each child.

Instruct each child in the following procedures:
- Trace Cloud Pattern onto white felt twice. Cut out clouds.
- Glue one felt cloud to the end of a length of ribbon (see sketch).
- Squeeze a line of glue around edge of cloud and place other cloud on top, matching edges.
- Outline one side of cloud with glitter glue. Allow to dry.

Enrichment Idea: Print a Bible verse on a small piece of paper and glue to the cloud. Dot glitter glue around Bible verse.

Bible Bits: God saved Noah and his family from the flood because he believed what God said. Noah showed his love for God by obeying Him. How can we show love to God?

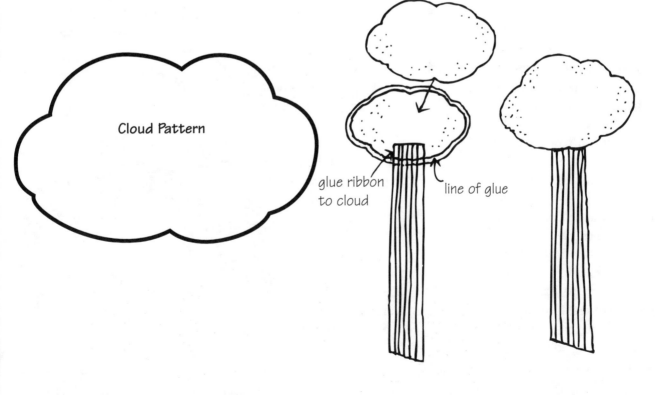

Cloud Pattern

glue ribbon to cloud

line of glue

RAINBOW REMINDER
(25-30 MINUTES)

Materials
- Rainbow Reminder Pattern
- tissue paper in blue, green, yellow and red
- yarn
- liquid starch

Standard Supplies
- chalkboard and chalk or butcher paper and felt pen
- photocopier
- white card stock
- colored construction paper
- pencils
- paintbrushes
- scissors
- hole punch
- measuring stick
- shallow containers
- newspaper

Preparation: Photocopy Rainbow Reminder Pattern onto card stock—one for each child. Letter "Trust in God's wisdom" or words from a Bible verse on chalkboard or butcher paper. Cut colored construction paper into 2×3-inch (5×7.5-cm) rectangles—four for each child. Cut yarn into 6-inch (15-cm) lengths—four for each child—and 20-inch (50-cm) lengths—one for each child. Cut or tear tissue paper into 2-inch (5-cm) pieces. Cover work area with newspaper. Pour small amounts of liquid starch into shallow containers.

Instruct each child in the following procedures:
- Cut out card-stock rainbow.
- Use hole punch to punch holes in rainbow where indicated on pattern.
- Use paintbrush to paint liquid starch on top rainbow row.
- Place pieces of blue tissue on top row, fitting within the lines on pattern or overlapping slightly for a blended effect.
- Brush starch onto next row and add green tissue paper in the same manner.
- Continue, adding a row of yellow tissue and a row of red tissue pieces. Allow to dry.
- If necessary, trim tissue paper edges even with rainbow pattern.
- Letter "Trust in God's wisdom" or words from a Bible verse on construction-paper rectangles—one or more words on each paper.
- Punch a hole at the top of each paper.
- Thread a short length of yarn through holes in papers and then, keeping words of verse in order, thread yarn through bottom holes in rainbow and secure each end of yarn with a knot.
- Thread a long length of yarn through each of the holes in the top of the rainbow and secure with a knot. Tie these two strands together in a bow.

Bible Bits: **What is your favorite color in the rainbow? God made all the colors of the rainbow. Even when it rained and rained and the flood covered the earth, God had a plan. He made sure that Noah, his family, and every animal were safe. After the flood, the plants grew again. The animals and people filled the earth again. So every time you see a rainbow, remember that God is wise and we can trust Him to take care of us.**

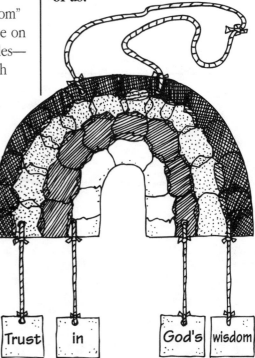

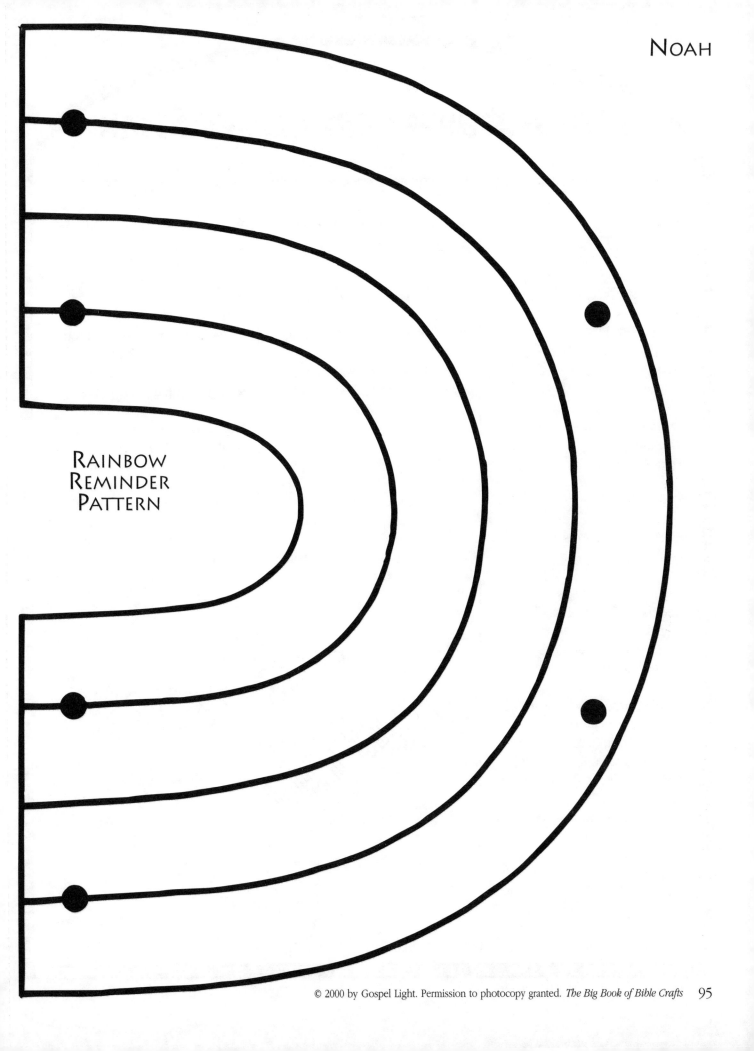

NOAH

RAINBOW
REMINDER
PATTERN

NOAH PUPPET OR PLANT STICK
(25-30 MINUTES)

Materials
- Noah Patterns
- Fun Foam in various colors including flesh tone, orange and white
- bamboo skewers

For each child—
- two jumbo craft sticks
- cotton ball
- three small wiggle eyes

Standard Supplies
- lightweight cardboard
- fine-tip felt pens including black and brown
- pencils
- craft glue
- heavy-duty scissors
- ruler

Preparation: Use scissors to cut skewers in half—one half for each child. Trace patterns onto lightweight cardboard and cut out two or three copies of each pattern.

Instruct each child in the following procedures:
- With pencil, trace Coat, Boots and Umbrella Patterns onto bright colors of Fun Foam. Cut out.
- Use felt pens to draw details on boots, umbrella and coat (sketch a).
- Trace Head and two Hand Patterns onto flesh-tone foam. Trace Giraffe Pattern onto orange foam and Dove onto white foam. Cut out.

- Draw details on giraffe with brown pen. Glue on one wiggle eye (sketch a).
- Glue two wiggle eyes onto Noah's face. Draw nose and eyebrows.
- Glue head to top of one craft stick. Then glue coat below head and boots below coat.
- Pull three small pieces of cotton from cotton ball and glue on top and on either side of head for hair (sketch a). Glue remaining cotton to face for beard.
- Glue hands behind sleeves (with thumbs up) and glue giraffe behind shoulder.
- Draw details on dove and glue to front of opposite shoulder.

- Overlapping 2 inches (5 cm), glue second craft stick to the back of the first craft stick (sketch b).
- Glue the bamboo skewer to the back of umbrella piece, with the point above umbrella top. Glue bottom of skewer to one hand.
- Lay Noah puppet flat until dry.

Bible Bits: **You can use your Noah puppet to tell the story of Noah and the ark, or you can place him in your favorite plant to decorate a room. If you had to take care of all the animals in the ark, which would be your favorite?**

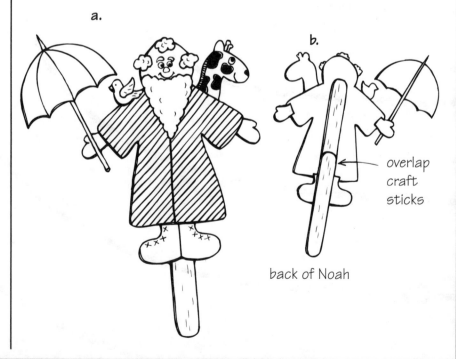

a.

b.

overlap craft sticks

back of Noah

NOAH PATTERNS

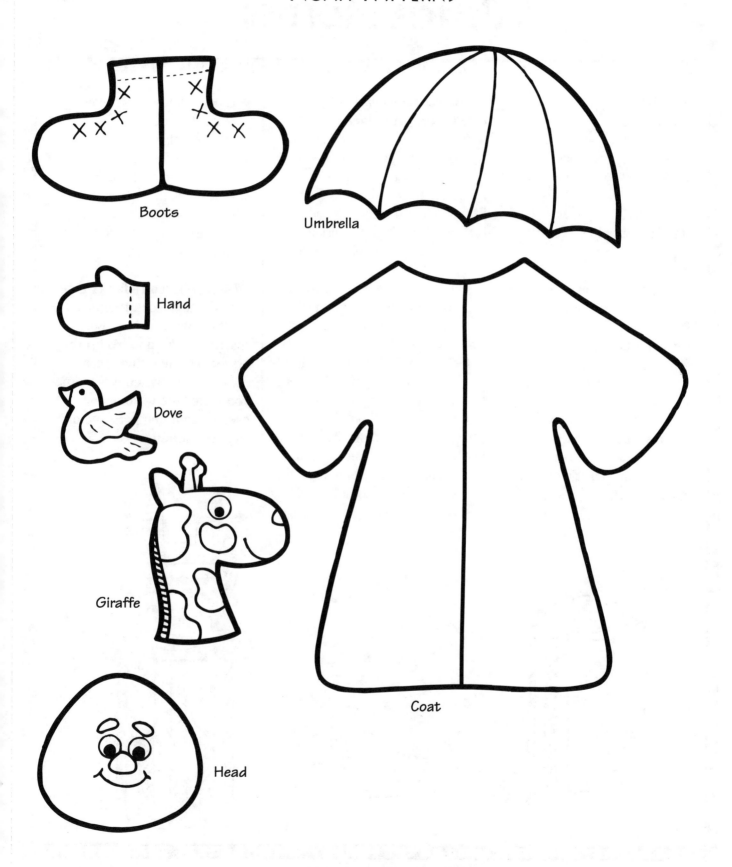

Boots

Umbrella

Hand

Dove

Giraffe

Coat

Head

"JOSEPH'S COAT" PENCIL HOLDER
(30-35 MINUTES)

Materials
- Joseph Patterns

For each child—
- one 12-oz. frozen juice can
- 20 chenille wires in various colors

Standard Supplies
- photocopier
- white card stock
- crayons in various colors including flesh tone
- craft glue
- sponge brushes
- scissors
- shallow containers

Preparation: Photocopy Joseph Patterns onto card stock—one copy for each child. Cut chenille wires in half. Pour glue into shallow containers.

Instruct each child in the following procedures:

- Brush glue on outside of can, one section at a time. Lay a chenille wire on glue with one end of wire even with the bottom of can. Bend top end of chenille wire to the inside of can and glue in place (sketch a).
- To make Joseph's coat, continue gluing different colors of chenille wires until entire can is covered.
- Color Joseph's face, neck, headdress and hands with crayons. Cut out.
- Cut and glue short pieces of chenille wire to the base of each hand for cuffs and across headdress for a band. Bend the ends of wires to backs of card stock (sketch b).

- Glue neck to upper inside front of can (sketch c).
- Make shepherd's crook by partially bending one end of a chenille wire over finger.
- Glue crook to front of body. Glue wrist of each hand to Joseph's coat, with one hand over crook.

Bible Bits: **Joseph's father gave him a special coat. Joseph's brothers were jealous. But Joseph was kind to his brothers even though they were mean to him. When was a time you were kind to someone even though that person didn't treat you kindly?**

a.

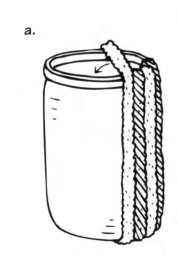

b.

hand

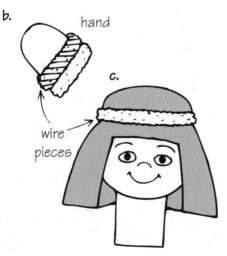

wire pieces

c.

JOSEPH PATTERNS

Head

Hands

MOSES KEY RING
(20-25 MINUTES)

Materials
- acrylic paints in peach, brown, blue and gray
- hand or power drill
- ⅛-inch (.3125-cm) drill bit
- black fine-tip permanent felt pen

For each child—
- one large, flat wooden clothespin (nonspring-type)
- one eye screw
- one split key ring

Standard Supplies
- small paintbrushes
- shallow containers
- newspaper

Preparation: Drill starter hole in top of each clothespin. Cover work area with newspaper. Pour acrylic paints into shallow containers.

Instruct each child in the following procedures:
- Paint lower portion of clothespin brown for body. Paint face peach, hair and beard gray and headdress blue. (See sketch.) Let dry.
- Add facial features and headband with felt pen.
- Screw eye screw into top of head.
- Attach key ring.

Enrichment Ideas: Children may make other Bible people. Hang several Bible characters together to make a mobile.

Bible Bits: **When Moses and the Israelites came to the Red Sea, what did God tell Moses to do?** (Hold up his staff.) **Moses had faith that God would help them escape from the Egyptians. But he also did his part by listening to God. We can have faith that God is with us, too. God also wants *us* to listen to Him and follow His instructions every day. How can we listen to God?** (Read the Bible, learn about Him at Sunday School or church, pray, etc.)

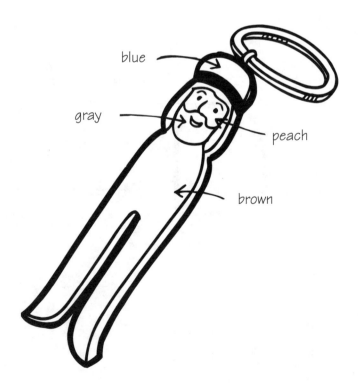

blue

gray

peach

brown

DAVID'S SHEEP
(20-30 MINUTES)

Materials
- small saw
- white cotton balls
- black felt
- black permanent felt pens

For each child—
- one large, flat wooden clothespin (nonspring-type)
- two craft sticks

Standard Supplies
- glue
- scissors
- craft knife
- ruler

Preparation: Cut ears and tails out of felt in the size and shape as shown in sketch a—two ears and one tail for each child. Use saw to cut prongs off clothespins (sketch b). Use craft knife to score and break craft sticks into three even pieces (sketch c). Discard middle piece of craft stick.

Instruct each child in the following procedures:
- Use black felt pen to color round head of wooden clothespin for sheep's head. Color rounded ends of four craft stick pieces to make feet.
- Tear two cotton balls in half. Gently stretch each half into a 2-inch (5-cm) strip.
- Glue cotton strip around each leg just above colored feet (sketch d).
- Glue legs onto clothespin body (sketch e). Make sure legs are even by standing sheep on a flat surface. Lay sheep on side to dry.
- Tear several cotton balls in half. Glue cotton pieces to clothespin until entire body of sheep is covered (sketch f).
- Glue one ear to each side of head. Glue tail onto rear of sheep's body (sketch f).

Enrichment Idea: If time allows, have each child make a flock of sheep.

Bible Bits: **David was a great king of Israel. But when he was young, he was a shepherd. He spent many hours watching and caring for his father's sheep. What do you think David did to take care of his sheep?**

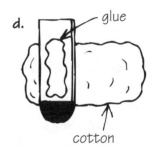
d.
glue
cotton

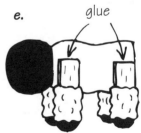
e.
glue

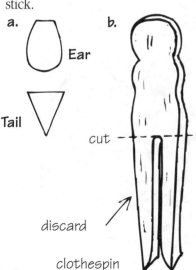
a.
Ear
Tail
b.
cut
discard
clothespin
c.
cut
discard
cut
craft stick

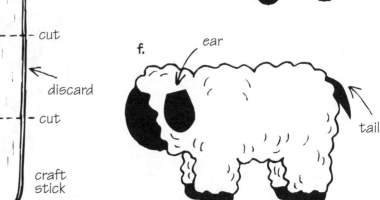
f.
ear
tail

"LITTLE LAMB" CAN
(25-30 MINUTES)

Materials
- Lamb Pattern
- small corkscrew pasta (rotini)
- white acrylic spray paint

For each child—
- one short cardboard can (such as a nut canister)
- two 20-mm wiggle eyes

Standard Supplies
- photocopier
- white card stock
- craft glue
- scissors
- newspaper

Preparation: Photocopy Lamb Pattern onto card stock—one for each child. Lay newspaper in a well-ventilated area and paint pasta and outsides of cans with white spray paint. Let dry.

Instruct each child in the following procedures:
- Cut out lamb's head.
- Glue two wiggle eyes on lamb's head.
- Glue rotini to the top of lamb's head where indicated on pattern. Lay flat to dry.
- Glue rotini all over can in random pattern. Break some of the rotini into shorter lengths for more variety.
- Glue the head to the outside of rotini-covered can (see sketch).

Bible Bits: David protected his sheep as he watched them. From what do you think David protected his sheep? (Lions, wolves, bears, falling from dangerous places, etc.) The Bible says that God is like a shepherd and we, His people, are like His sheep. It's good to know that God is always watching over us and protecting us, too.

LAMB PATTERN

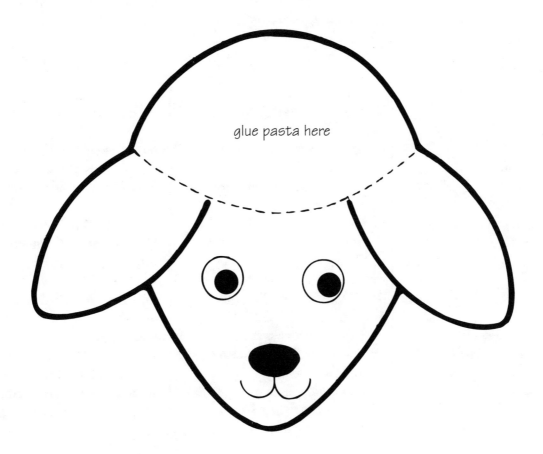

glue pasta here

"SHADRACH, MESHACH AND ABEDNEGO" POP-UP

(40-45 MINUTES)

Materials
- small rubber bands
- fabric scraps

For each child—
- one half-gallon milk carton
- one tongue depressor
- four wooden craft spoons
- six small wiggle eyes

Standard Supplies
- construction paper in yellow, red and orange
- black fine-tip felt pens
- craft glue
- scissors
- ruler

Preparation: Cut milk cartons to stand 4 inches (10 cm) high (sketch a). Cut a 1-inch (2.5-cm) slit in the bottom center of each milk carton (sketch a). Cut construction paper into 5×12-inch (12.5×30-cm) rectangles—one of each color for each child. Cut fabric scraps into 2×3-inch (5×7.5-cm) rectangles—three for each child.

Instruct each child in the following procedures:
- Wrap and glue fabric scraps onto three wooden spoons for headdresses. Secure to spoon with small rubber bands as headbands (sketch b).
- Glue two wiggle eyes onto each of the three wooden spoons.
- Use felt pens to draw nose and mouth on each spoon.
- Glue tongue depressor and wooden spoons together as shown in sketch c. Let dry.
- Cut construction-paper rectangles into 5-inch (12.5-cm) flames approximately 1 inch (2.5 cm) wide (sketch d).
- Fold some flames (sketch e) and glue around top inside milk carton (sketch f).
- On outside, glue six to eight flames around all four sides of milk carton (sketch g).

- Place tongue depressor through slot in bottom of milk carton and pull Shadrach, Meshach and Abednego inside the fiery furnace. Move the tongue depressor up to make the men come out of the fire unharmed!

Enrichment Idea: Letter Daniel 3:26 on construction paper and glue to front of fiery furnace.

Bible Bits: **Why were Shadrach, Meshach and Abednego thrown into the fiery furnace?** (They would not bow down and worship King Nebuchadnezzar's statue.) **Shadrach, Meshach and Abednego knew that they should worship only the one true God. They loved God and wanted to obey Him, even if they faced danger!**

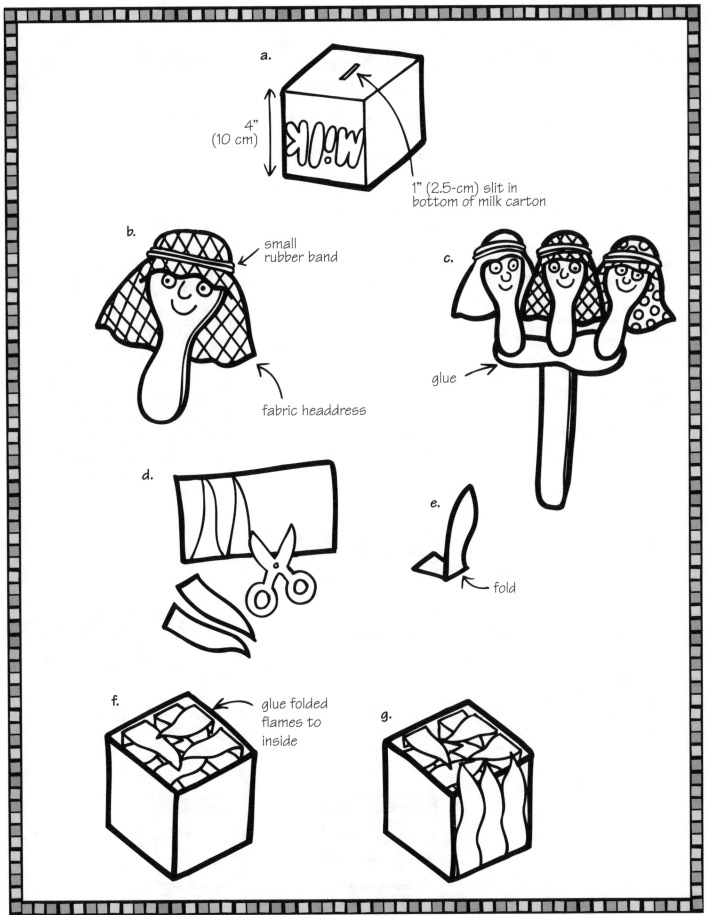

a.

4"
(10 cm)

MILK

1" (2.5-cm) slit in
bottom of milk carton

b.

small
rubber band

fabric headdress

c.

glue

d.

e.

fold

f.

glue folded
flames to
inside

g.

"FIERY FURNACE" CANDLE
(20-25 MINUTES)

Materials
- table salt
- candlewick
- dry tempera paints in black, red, orange and yellow
- paraffin wax
- spoons
- bamboo skewers
- empty coffee can
- stove or hot plate
- saucepan
- measuring utensils

For each child—
- one clean baby-food jar

Standard Supplies
- scissors
- ruler
- four shallow containers
- water

Preparation: Cut candlewick into 3-inch (7.5-cm) lengths. Pour 1 cup of salt into each shallow container. Mix 1 teaspoon dry tempera into each container of salt to make four colors. (Add more tempera for greater color intensity.) Melt wax in a can set in a saucepan of water. Heat on low. (Watch closely as wax will melt quickly.)

Instruct each child in the following procedures:
- Spoon layers of red, orange and yellow salt into the jar.
- Add a final layer of black salt, stopping 1 inch (2.5 cm) from top of jar (sketch a).
- Press a skewer against the inside of the jar and push skewer down through all salt layers. Carefully pull skewer out and repeat procedure around the sides of the jar to make "flames" (sketch b).
- Push the wick down through the middle of the salt (sketch c).

- With adult supervision, carefully pour the hot wax into the jar, filling it to the top (sketch c).
- Allow wax to harden.
- Trim wick if necessary.

Bible Bits: **What is a furnace?** (Children respond. They may mention fireplaces or furnaces that heat their houses.) **In the Bible, the fiery furnace that Shadrach, Meshach and Abednego were thrown into was probably used as a huge kiln to fire pottery. Even though they faced death in the fire, Shadrach, Meshach and Abednego showed their faith in God by obeying Him.**

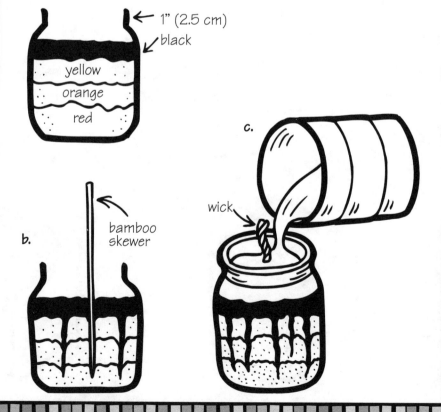

a.

← 1" (2.5 cm)

↙ black

yellow

orange

red

b.

bamboo skewer

c.

wick

POM-POM LION
(15-20 MINUTES)

Materials
- brown bump chenille wire
- yellow chenille wire

For each child—
- two 1-inch (2.5-cm) yellow pom-poms
- five ½-inch (1.25-cm) yellow pom-poms
- two ¼-inch (.625-cm) yellow pom-poms
- one 1-inch (2.5-cm) yellow tinsel pom-pom
- one ⅛-inch (.3125-cm) brown pom-pom
- two small wiggle eyes

Standard Supplies
- craft glue
- scissors
- ruler

Preparation: Cut bumps in brown chenille wire apart—one bump for each child. Cut yellow chenille wire into 3-inch (7.5-cm) pieces—one piece for each child.

Instruct each child in the following procedures:
- Glue two large pom-poms together to make lion body.
- Glue four medium-size pom-poms to body to make feet.
- Make tail by bending one end of yellow chenille wire around the middle of the brown chenille bump (sketch a). Twist chenille bump ends together. Glue tail to lion body.
- On tinsel pom-pom, glue two small yellow pom-poms to make ears. Glue on wiggle eyes. Below eyes, glue remaining medium-size yellow pom-pom. Glue on brown pom-pom to make nose (sketch b).
- Glue head onto lion body. Allow glue to dry.

Bible Bits: Daniel was a trusted helper to the king, and the king appreciated Daniel. When some men plotted to get rid of Daniel, the king was very upset. Even though Daniel was thrown into the lions' den, the king hoped that Daniel's God would save him. How did God save Daniel? (He sent an angel who shut the lions' mouths.) **Why do you think God saved Daniel?**

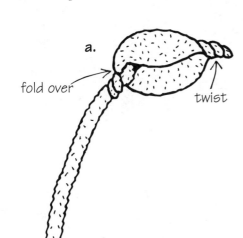

a.

fold over

twist

b.

The Big Book of Bible Crafts

LION CRAYON HOLDER
(20-25 MINUTES)

Materials
- yellow poster board
- gold acrylic spray paint
- small corkscrew pasta (rotini)

For each child—
- one short cardboard can (such as a nut canister)
- two 20-mm wiggle eyes

Standard Supplies
- yellow construction paper
- black felt pen
- pencil
- craft glue
- scissors
- ruler
- newspaper

Preparation: Cut poster board into 5-inch (12.5-cm) circles—one for each child. Cut construction paper into rectangles large enough to wrap around each can—one for each child. Lay newspaper in a well-ventilated area and spray paint pasta gold. Let dry.

Instruct each child in the following procedures:
- Glue eyes onto yellow circle.
- Use felt pen to draw nose, whiskers and mouth of lion (sketch a).
- Glue ends of pasta around circle to make a mane (sketch c). Allow glue to dry.
- Draw feet on construction paper strip.
- Spread glue on back of construction paper strip and wrap around can (sketch b).
- Glue head onto can (sketch c). Hold in place until glue is dry.

Bible Bits: When was a time you saw a real lion? Lions can be dangerous if they aren't in a cage. Daniel was thrown into the lions' den because he would not pray to the king. He knew he should pray only to God. Because Daniel was brave and obeyed God, God saved Daniel.

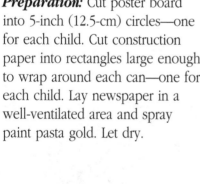

a.

b.

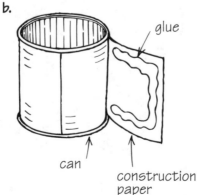

glue

can

construction paper

c.

"JONAH AND THE BIG FISH" SHADOWBOX
(35-45 MINUTES)

Materials
◆ Big Fish Pattern
◆ blue poster board
◆ fabric scraps
◆ tissue-paper scraps

For each child—
◆ one empty cookie, cracker or small cereal box
◆ one wooden craft spoon
◆ two small wiggle eyes

Standard Supplies
◆ construction paper
◆ black felt pens
◆ pencils
◆ glue
◆ hot-glue gun and glue sticks
◆ scissors
◆ ruler

Preparation: Enlarge Big Fish Pattern to cover boxes. Trace pattern onto blue poster board and cut out—one for each child. Cut fin where indicated on pattern. Cut construction paper into 2×5-inch (5×12.5-cm) lengths—one for each child. Cut out an opening in the center section of each box (sketch a). Plug in glue gun out of reach of children.

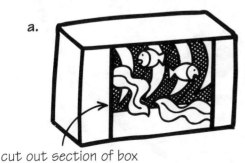

a.

cut out section of box

Instruct each child in the following procedures:
◆ Imagine what Jonah saw inside the big fish. Inside opening of box, glue on tissue-paper scraps to create a scene that looks like what Jonah saw (sketch a).
◆ With felt pens, draw hair, beard and facial features on wooden spoon to make Jonah figure. Glue on wiggle eyes (sketch b).
◆ Cut and glue fabric onto spoon for clothing.
◆ Cut out a conversation balloon from construction paper. Write what Jonah might have said while inside the big fish (sketch c).

b.

wiggle eyes

wooden craft spoon

◆ With teacher's help, use glue gun to glue Jonah to the back side of cutout opening of fish (sketch d).
◆ Glue the conversation balloon to back side of opening to look like Jonah is talking (sketch d).
◆ Use felt pen to draw eye and mouth onto big fish. Glue the fish onto box, with scene under fin.
◆ Fold back fin to see Jonah.

Bible Bits: **Jonah didn't want to tell God's message to the people in Nineveh. So he ran away from God and ended up in the belly of a big fish! What do you think it was like inside the fish's belly?** (Children respond.) **What do you think Jonah thought while he was inside the fish?** Read Jonah 2:1-3,7,9.

c.

d.

glue Jonah and conversation balloon to back of fish

BIG FISH PATTERN

cut here

cut here

BIBLE CHARACTER DOLL
(20-25 MINUTES)

Materials
- heavy yarn in various colors including brown and black
- fabric

For each child—
- one plastic individual-size drink bottle
- one 3-inch (7.5-cm) Styrofoam ball
- two large wiggle eyes

Optional—
- sand

Standard Supplies
- felt pens
- craft glue
- scissors
- measuring stick

Preparation: Remove lids from bottles. (*Optional:* Fill bottles with sand for stability.) Use one bottle to gently push the bottle neck into each Styrofoam ball to make indentation. Cut fabric into 7×15-inch (17.5×37.5-cm) rectangles. Cut neck opening in center of fabric (sketch a).

Instruct each child in the following procedures:
- Place hole in fabric over neck of bottle (sketch b).
- Squeeze glue into indentation in Styrofoam ball and insert bottle neck into indentation.
- With felt pens, draws nose, mouth and cheeks on Styrofoam ball to make face.
- Glue on wiggle eyes.
- Cut and glue brown or black yarn to head for hair and/or beard.
- Cut a long length of yarn and tie around waist for belt.

Bible Bits: **Which person in our Bible story did you make? What did you learn about that person?**

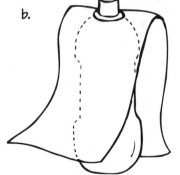

a.

b.

The Big Book of Bible Crafts

BIBLE PEOPLE PUPPETS
(30-35 MINUTES)

Materials
- Bible People Puppet Patterns
- Fun Foam in various colors including flesh tone and hair shades
- ¼-inch (.625-cm) ribbon
- red and black fine-tip permanent felt pens

For each child—
- two 7-mm wiggle eyes
- one jumbo craft stick

Standard Supplies
- lightweight cardboard
- pencil
- pens
- craft glue
- scissors

Preparation: Trace Bible People Puppet Patterns onto lightweight cardboard and cut out. Make several copies of each pattern.

Instruct each child in the following procedures:
- Trace Bible People Patterns onto Fun Foam. Use different patterns as desired for specific Bible characters. Trace face pattern onto flesh-tone colored foam, hair and/or beard patterns onto hair-colored foam, and headdresses onto brightly colored foam. Cut out.
- Use black felt pen to draw details on hair (such as curly or wavy lines) or headdress.
- Glue face piece onto one end of craft stick.
- Glue front hair, beard and/or headdress onto face piece (sketch a).
- Glue back of hair or headdress onto back of craft stick and face piece (sketch b).
- Cut a short piece of ribbon and glue across head for headband, if desired (sketch c).
- With red felt pen draw mouth on face.
- Glue two wiggle eyes on face.
- Use black felt pen to write the name of your Bible character on the craft stick.

Bible Bits: Which Bible person did you make, (Charlie)? Find friends who made the other characters in your story. Then together you can tell us the story using your puppets!

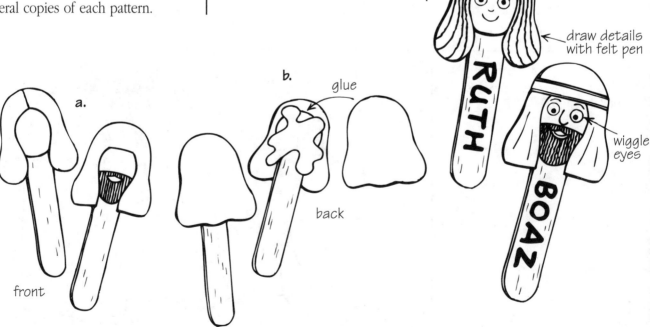

c.

ribbon

draw details with felt pen

wiggle eyes

b.

glue

back

a.

front

BIBLE PEOPLE PATTERNS

Face

Long Hair Front

Medium Hair Front

Short Hair Front

Long Hair and Headdress Back

Medium Hair and Headdress Back

Short Hair and Headdress Back

Medium Headdress Front

Long Headdress Front

Beard

The Big Book of Bible Crafts 113

"THE THREE KINGS AND STAR" PUPPETS

(40-50 MINUTES)

Materials

- ¼-inch (.625-cm) wooden dowels
- saw
- brown chenille wire
- poster board in silver, gold or yellow
- paper twist in metallic and various colors
- yarn in various colors including gray, black and brown
- gold star garland
- sequins, acrylic jewels or beads
- black fine-tip permanent felt pens

For each child—

- six 5-inch (12.5-cm) wooden spoons
- two 12-mm wiggle eyes
- six 5-mm wiggle eyes

Standard Supplies

- brown felt pens
- pencil
- craft glue
- scissors
- measuring stick

Preparation: Use saw to cut wooden dowels into 10-inch (25-cm) lengths. Glue two wooden spoons together, end to end, for puppet body (sketch a)—three pairs of spoons for each child. Cut paper twist into 8-inch (20-cm) lengths—at least three lengths for each child. Cut gold star garland into 20-inch (50-cm) lengths—one for each child. Draw a 6-inch (15-cm) star pattern on poster board for each child and cut out. Save poster-board scraps.

Instruct each child in the following procedures:
To make the three kings:

- Color one rounded spoon end of each puppet with a brown felt pen to make puppets' heads.
- For arms, glue chenille wire on back of spoon bodies below heads. Wrap wire around neck once and then twist together in back (sketch b).
- To make hands, bend each wire end back ½ inch (1.25 cm).
- Untwist all paper twist and smooth out.
- For each robe, fold one piece of paper twist in half and cut a 1—inch (2.5-cm) slit in the center of fold (sketch c). Slip the head of puppet through the slit.
- For belts, cut lengths of yarn and wrap around waists and tie.
- For hair and beards, cut gray, black or brown yarn into small pieces and glue onto heads of puppets.
- Cut smaller pieces of metallic paper twist for crowns. Crowns can be cut into points, glued at an angle or decorated with sequins, jewels or beads to look different from one another. Wrap crowns around heads and glue to secure.

- Glue on small wiggle eyes.
- Use felt pen to draw other facial features.
- For gifts, cut poster-board scraps into 1-inch (2.5-cm) squares. Wrap with paper twist and glue on a sequin, jewel or bead to decorate.
- Fold chenille-wire arms around gifts and glue in place (sketch d).

To make the star:

- Glue large wiggle eyes on star. Use black felt pen to draw eyebrows and mouth.
- Glue gold star garland around outside edge of star (sketch e).
- For handle, glue wooden dowel on back side of star. Allow to dry.

Bible Bits: **Where did the three kings travel from?** (The East.) **They followed the star a long time and for many miles before they finally got to see Jesus. The three kings traveled far because they knew Jesus was the Son of God and wanted to worship Him. How can we worship Jesus now?** (Pray, sing, learn about Him in church and Sunday School, etc.)

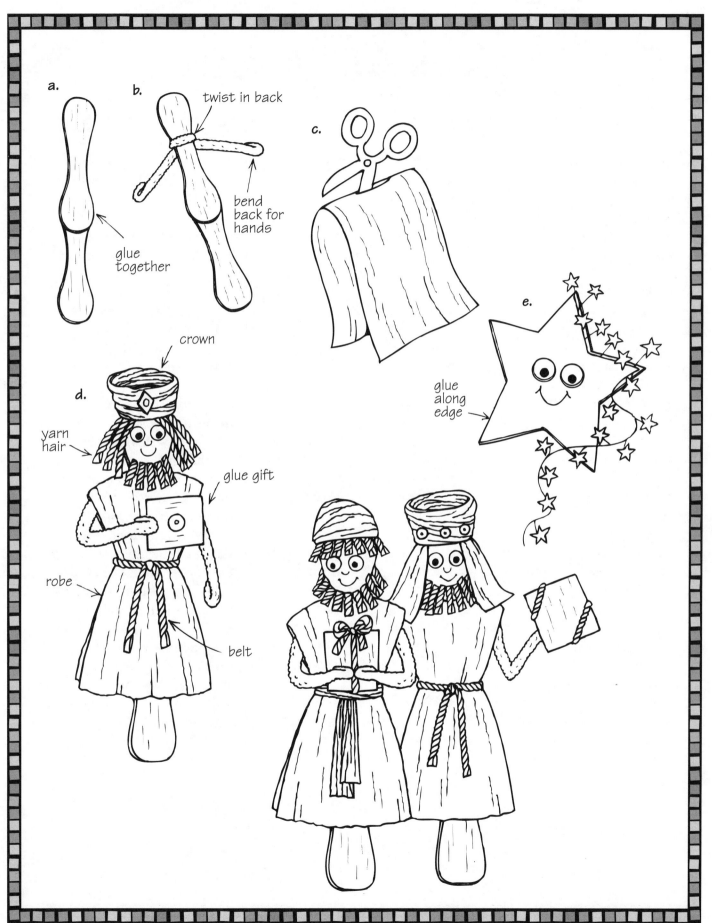

a.

glue together

b.

twist in back

bend back for hands

c.

d.

crown

yarn hair

glue gift

robe

belt

e.

glue along edge

PAPER-BAG ANGEL
(25-30 MINUTES)

Materials
- Angel and Wing Patterns
- paper grocery bags
- narrow ribbon
- buttons or sequins
- silver or gold chenille wire
- glitter glue
- pinking shears or decorative edging scissors

Standard Supplies
- lightweight cardboard
- colored felt pens
- pencils
- glue sticks
- craft glue
- scissors
- ruler
- paper clips

Preparation: Trace Angel and Wing Patterns onto cardboard and cut out several copies of each pattern. Cut paper bags into pieces large enough to fit patterns—three pieces for each child. Cut ribbon into 8-inch (20-cm) and 4-inch (10-cm) lengths—one of each length for each child. Cut chenille wires into 8-inch (20-cm) lengths—one for each child.

Instruct each child in the following procedures:
- Trace Angel Pattern onto paper bag. Cut out.
- Use glue stick to apply a line of glue along all edges of angel on printed side of paper (sketch a).
- Press glued side of angel onto printed side of another piece of paper bag.
- Use pinking shears or decorative edging scissors to cut along edge of first angel cutout, cutting away excess paper.
- Trace Wing Pattern onto paper bag.
- Use pinking shears or decorative edging scissors to cut out wings.
- Use felt pens to draw facial features and hair on angel.
- For tie around neck, center 4-inch (10-cm) length of ribbon across back of neck and cross ribbon in front. Glue in place (sketch b).
- Glue paper clip to back of head.
- Decorate angel's robe with glitter glue and/or glue on buttons or sequins as desired.
- Fold wings on lines shown on pattern and glue to back of angel (sketch c). Decorate with glitter glue as desired.
- To make halo, curve chenille wire into halo shape and twist stem (sketch d). Glue halo to back of head.
- Thread 8-inch (20-cm) length of ribbon through paper-clip hanger. Tie ends together in knot (sketch e). Trim ends.

Bible Bits: **Angels announced the birth of Jesus to shepherds who were watching their sheep. What would you have thought if you had been one of those shepherds?** (Children respond.) **They must have looked a little afraid, because the first thing an angel said to them was "Do not be afraid. I bring you good news of great joy that will be for all the people."** (Luke 2:10.) **Why is it such good news that Jesus came to earth?** (Jesus came to tell us about God's love for us. He died and rose again, so we can be with God forever.)

a.

b. ribbon

c. glue to back

folds

d. paper clip

glue stem

e. tie ribbon

buttons

glitter glue

Jesus' Birth

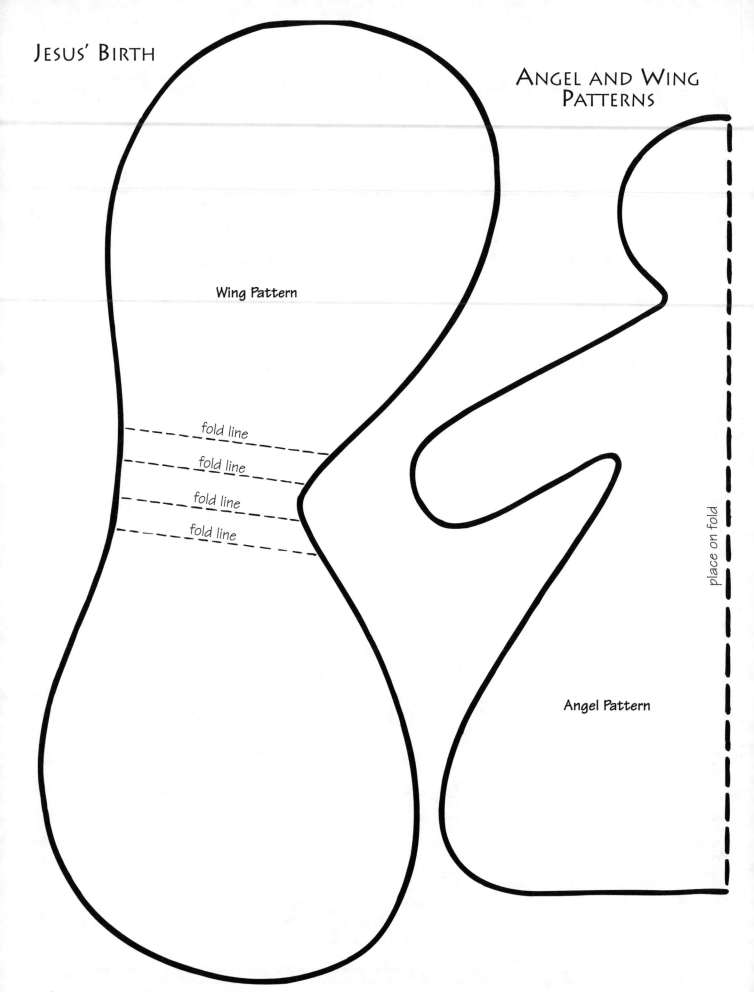

Wing Pattern

fold line

fold line

fold line

fold line

place on fold

Angel Pattern

SEASHELL ANGEL ORNAMENT
(25-30 MINUTES)

Materials
◆ ⅛-inch (.3125-cm) satin ribbon
◆ curly doll hair
◆ tiny shells
◆ black and red fine-tip perma-nent felt pens

For each child—
◆ one medium-sized scallop or other fan-shaped shell
◆ one small bowl-shaped shell (such as small clamshell)
◆ one 16-mm fake pearl

Standard Supplies
◆ craft glue
◆ hot-glue gun and glue sticks
◆ scissors
◆ ruler

Preparation: Cut ribbon into 12-inch (30-cm) lengths—two for each child. Plug in glue gun out of reach of children.

Instruct each child in the following procedures:
◆ With teacher's help, apply hot glue to the edge of the pointed end of bowl-shaped shell. Glue to the larger scallop shell as shown in sketch a.
◆ Wrap a ribbon around neck of shell angel and tie in a knot or bow (sketch a).
◆ Slide the other length of ribbon through the neck ribbon at the back of angel. Tie around neck ribbon and then knot ends together to make a hanging loop (sketch b).
◆ Glue ribbon loop to the back of the small shell, so angel will hang upright.
◆ On pearl, use black felt pen to draw dots for eyes and eye-brows. Use red felt pen to draw mouth and cheeks (sketch c).

◆ Glue pearl to the inside of small shell.
◆ Cut a small amount of doll hair and glue around pearl for hair.
◆ Glue tiny shells on angel robe or "halo" to decorate, if desired. Allow to dry.

Bible Bits: **How did Jesus' mother, Mary, find out she was going to have a baby who would be God's Son?** (An angel told her.) **Who else heard about Jesus' birth from angels?** (The shepherds. Joseph.) **When Jesus was born, it was very good news. God sent Jesus to tell us about God's love for us. God loves us so much He sent His Son to earth to live and die so that we can be with God forever!**

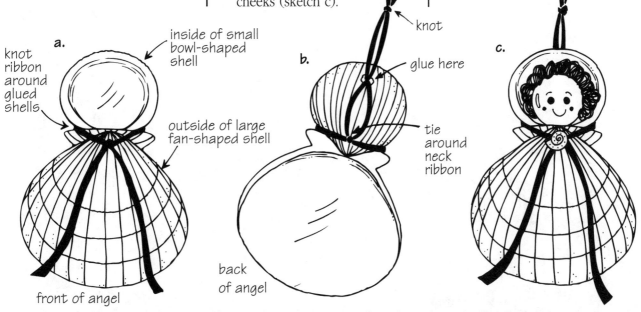

a.
knot ribbon around glued shells
inside of small bowl-shaped shell
outside of large fan-shaped shell
front of angel

b.
knot
glue here
tie around neck ribbon
back of angel

c.

Spool Stable Animals
(15-20 minutes)

Materials
- Spool Stable Animal Patterns
- empty plastic thread spools (or toilet-paper tubes cut in half)
- yarn
- cotton balls
- black, pink and brown felt

Standard Supplies
- photocopier
- white card stock
- crayons or felt pens
- pen
- scissors
- glue sticks
- ruler

Preparation: Choose one or more animals for each child to make. Photocopy Spool Stable Animal Patterns onto card stock—one for each child. For pig or donkey, cut pink or brown felt into 1½×4-inch (3.75×10-cm) strips—one felt strip for each animal made. Cut yarn into 2-inch (5-cm) lengths for donkey or pig tails.

Instruct each child in the following procedures:
- Color animal front and back. Cut out.
- Trace animal ear patterns onto felt. Use brown felt for donkey, black felt for sheep and pink felt for pig. Cut out ears.
- Glue yarn piece or cotton ball to animal back for tail.
- Glue ears to animal's head.
- Glue a cotton ball between sheep's ears (sketch a).
- Apply glue stick to the spool. Wrap felt strip around glued spool for donkey or pig (sketch b). Press cotton balls to spool for sheep.
- Apply glue stick to the ends of spool. Then press front and back body pieces to spool (sketch b).

Enrichment Idea: Children glue wiggle eyes to animals.

Bible Bits: **The night that Jesus was born, Bethlehem was very crowded. So what did Mary and Joseph do?** (They asked to stay in an innkeeper's stable.) **What do you think it smelled like in the stable? What animals do you think were there?**

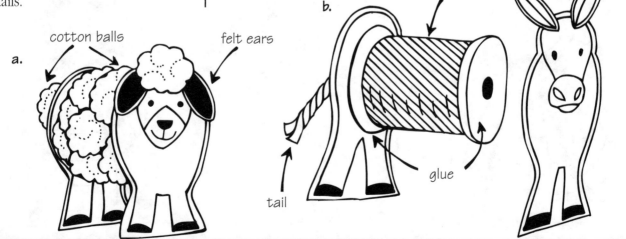

a. cotton balls   felt ears

b.   felt   glue   tail

SPOOL STABLE ANIMAL PATTERNS

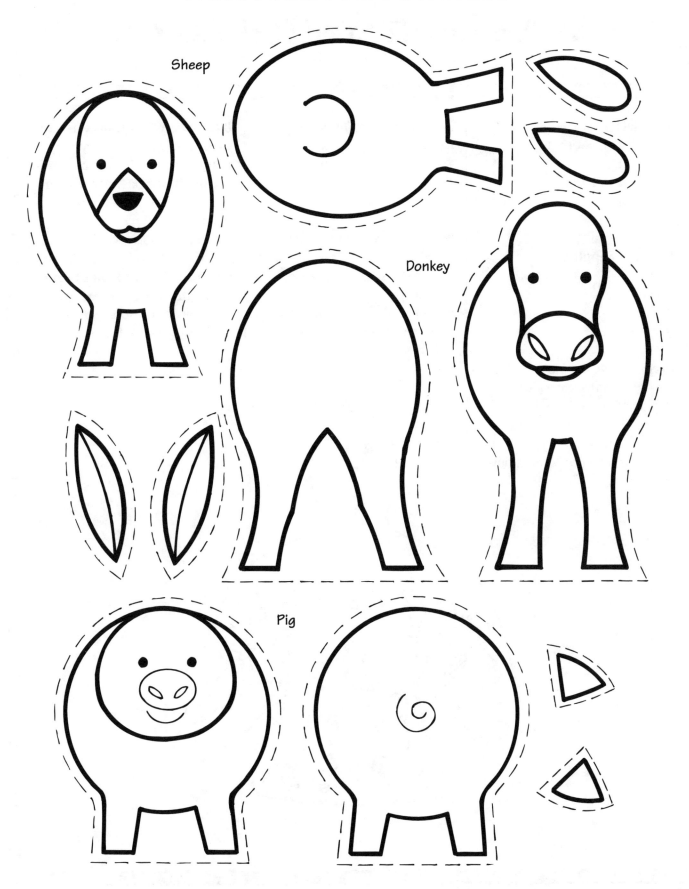

Sheep

Donkey

Pig

DOVE LIGHT-SWITCH COVER
(15-20 MINUTES)

Materials
- Dove Light-Switch Cover Pattern
- white Fun Foam
- fabric paints in squeeze bottles
- nails

Standard Supplies
- pen
- scissors
- ruler
- newspaper

Preparation: Cut Fun Foam into 8-inch (20-cm) squares—one for each child. Trace Dove Light-Switch Cover Pattern onto each square. Mark screw holes and cut out switch opening on each dove.

Instruct each child in the following procedures:
- Cut out Fun Foam dove.
- Use a nail to poke through the two marks for the light-switch screws.
- Decorate your dove with fabric paint as desired. Make dots for dove eyes and squiggles for feathers.
- Allow light-switch covers to dry overnight before attaching to light switch.

Bible Bits: When Jesus was baptized, God showed everyone that Jesus was His Son by sending the Holy Spirit in the form of a dove. What did a voice from heaven say? ("You are my Son, whom I love; with you I am well pleased." [Luke 3:22.]) **When you turn on your light in your room, this dove will remind you that Jesus, God's Son, came to show us God's love.**

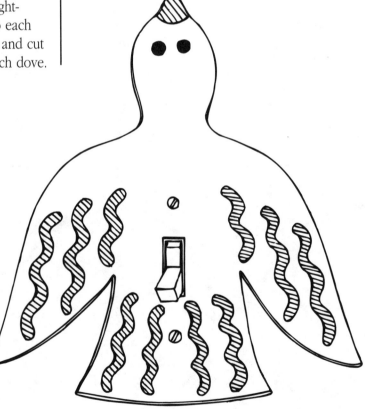

DOVE LIGHT-SWITCH COVER PATTERN

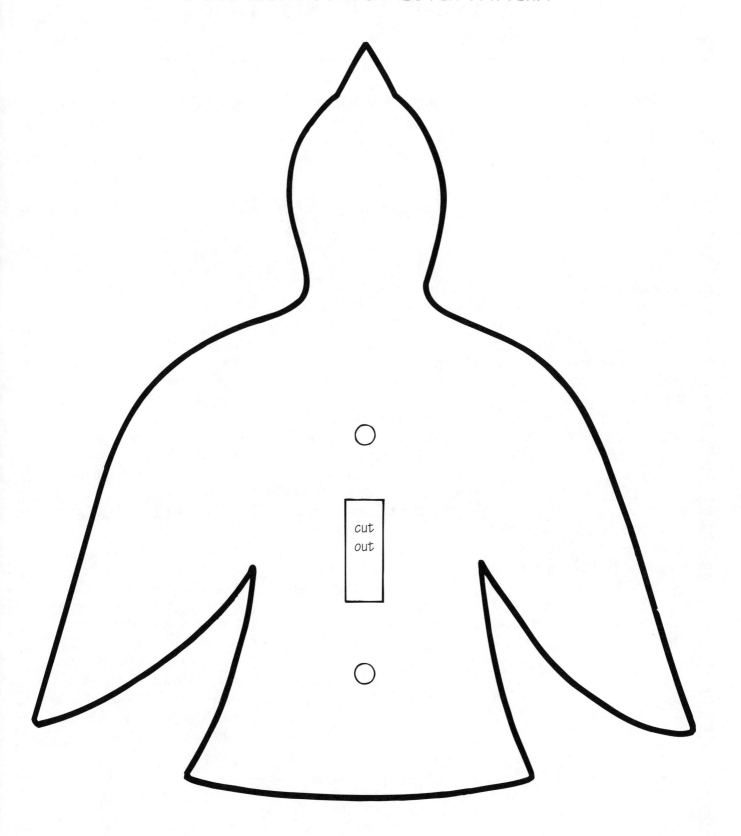

cut
out

DISCIPLE MUSEUM
(30-35 MINUTES)

Materials
- chenille wire in various colors including tan
- burlap and fabric scraps
- assorted decorating materials (twigs, netting, fish crackers, etc.)
- yarn
- modeling clay
- white poster board

For each child—
- one round-head wooden clothespin

Standard Supplies
- fine- and wide-tip felt pens
- glue
- scissors
- ruler

Preparation: Cut burlap and other fabric scraps into 3×6-inch (7.5×15-cm) rectangles for robes and 1½×3½-inch (3.75×8.75-cm) rectangles for headpieces—one of each for each child. Cut poster board into 6×12-inch (15×30-cm) rectangles and 1×3-inch (2.5×7.5-cm) strips—one of each for each child.

Instruct each child in the following procedures:
- Choose one of Jesus' disciples with whom you are familiar.
- Center and wrap tan chenille wire below the head of a clothespin for the disciple's arms.
- Choose a 3×6-inch (7.5×15-cm) piece of burlap or fabric for the disciple's robe.
- Fold fabric in half. Cut a slit in fold to allow clothespin head to fit through. Slip robe over head (sketch a).
- Squeeze a little glue onto clothespin body to secure robe to clothespin. Tie a length of yarn around robe at waist.
- Use felt pens to draw the disciple's face on the clothespin.
- Glue small pieces of yarn on head of clothespin to make hair and/or beard (sketch b).
- Glue the 1½×3½-inch (3.75×8.75-cm) piece of burlap or fabric to top of head and tie in place with yarn around forehead.
- Roll a piece of clay to form a ball. Stick the bottom of clothespin into ball and set on table to make a stand, flattening the bottom of clay slightly (sketch c).
- Fold the large poster-board piece in half.
- On the front of poster board, draw and color a scene or place that your disciple could be (at a lake fishing, under a tree, walking down a road, in a town, etc.).
- If desired, glue materials on your scene such as netting for fish net, small fish-shaped crackers for fish, twigs for wood or branches of trees, etc.
- Bend each end of poster-board strip ½ inch (1.25 cm) to make tabs. Glue tabs inside the poster-board backdrop to make stand (sketch d).
- Set your disciple in front of the scene.
- Now walk through our disciple museum. See and learn about Jesus' other disciples.

Bible Bits: Which disciple are you making? What do you remember about him? Why do you think Jesus picked him as a disciple?

cut slit

a.

chenille wire arms

b.

fabric

c.

yarn

yarn

clay

d.

tab

ZACCHAEUS, YOU COME DOWN
(25-30 MINUTES)

Materials
- Zacchaeus and Treetop Patterns
- green Fun Foam or poster board
- brown Fun Foam or construction paper
- brown yarn
- craft knife

For each child—
- two wooden beads

Standard Supplies
- photocopier
- white card stock
- pencil
- felt pens
- masking tape
- scissors
- hole punch
- measuring stick

Preparation: Photocopy Zacchaeus Pattern onto card stock—one for each child. Trace Treetop Pattern onto green Fun Foam or poster board and cut out—one for each child. Use felt pen to mark a dot where holes are to be punched in treetop (as indicated on pattern). Use craft knife to cut slits in treetop for doorknob opening (sketch a). Cut yarn into 4-foot (1.2-m) lengths— one for each child. Cut brown Fun Foam or construction paper into tree trunk shapes, 2×11 inches (5×27.5 cm)—one for each child.

Instruct each child in the following procedures:
- Use felt pens to draw and color Zacchaeus's face, hair and clothes.
- Cut out Zacchaeus and punch holes where indicated.
- Punch holes in treetop where indicated.
- Outline treetop with a felt pen and draw tree details, birds, etc., if desired.
- Wrap a small piece of masking tape around one end of yarn to make sewing tip. Tie a double knot at opposite end of yarn.
- Thread one bead onto yarn and pull to the knotted end of yarn. Make sure knot is big enough to hold the bead in place.
- Lay cutouts on table with Zacchaeus below the treetop. Thread yarn tip through the holes in Zacchaeus and in treetop as shown in sketch b.
- Thread the second bead onto the yarn. Cut off masking tape tip and tie a double knot to secure bead.
- Glue tree trunk to the back of treetop, below the doorknob cutout. Allow to dry.
- Place treetop opening over doorknob. Slide Zacchaeus to the treetop. Alternately pull down on each side of yarn to watch Zacchaeus climb down (sketch c), or gently pull yarn to the sides to watch Zacchaeus climb up.

Bible Bits: **Nobody in town liked Zacchaeus. He made them pay more tax money than they had to and then he kept the extra money for himself! Zacchaeus wasn't truthful. But after he met Jesus, he wanted to give back all the money he took and more. Zacchaeus wanted to change and be truthful because Jesus showed love to him. When someone loves you, even when you do something wrong, how do you feel?** (Children respond.) **God loves you all the time, and He wants you to be truthful, too.**

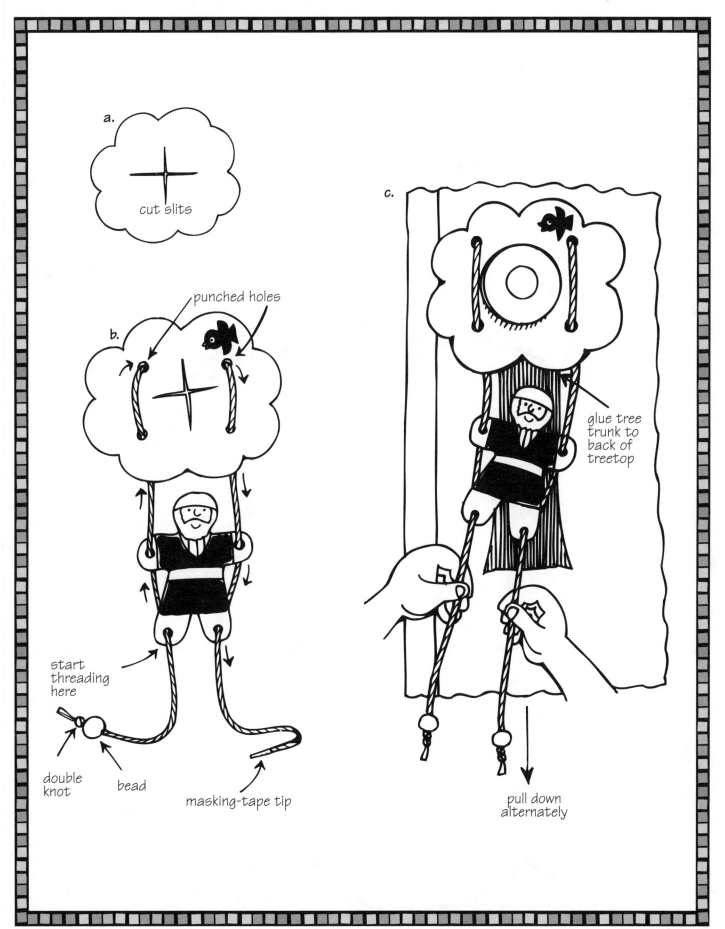

a.

cut slits

punched holes

b.

start
threading
here

double
knot

bead

masking-tape tip

c.

glue tree
trunk to
back of
treetop

pull down
alternately

Zacchaeus Pattern

Treetop Pattern

cut here

cut here

"PETER'S BOAT" BOOKMARK

(10-15 MINUTES)

Materials
◆ Boat and Fish Patterns
◆ yarn

Standard Supplies
◆ photocopier
◆ white card stock
◆ felt pens
◆ craft glue
◆ scissors
◆ ruler

Preparation: Cut yarn into 10-inch (25-cm) lengths—one for each child. Photocopy Boat and Fish Patterns onto card stock—two of each for each child.

Instruct each child in the following procedures:
◆ Using felt pens, color the front and back of Boat and Fish Patterns.
◆ Cut out patterns.
◆ Glue the back and front of boat together, with covered sides out and one end of yarn in between.
◆ Glue the two sides of fish together with the other end of yarn in between.
◆ Allow glue to dry before using your bookmark.

Bible Bits: What did Peter say to Jesus when Jesus told him to put out his fishing net again? ("Master, we've worked hard all night and haven't caught anything. But because you say so, I will let down the nets." [Luke 5:5.]) **What happened then?** (Peter caught so many fish, the net broke.) **Peter recognized then that Jesus was from God. He left everything to follow Jesus and became His disciple.**

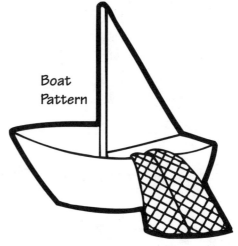

Boat Pattern

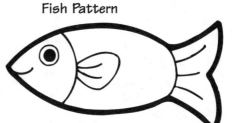

Fish Pattern

Happy Healed Man
(20-25 minutes)

Materials
- Body, Feet and Hand Patterns
- large, wide rubber bands
- yarn in brown, black or gray

Standard Supplies
- photocopier
- white card stock
- crayons or felt pens
- glue
- stapler and staples
- scissors
- hole punch
- measuring stick

Preparation: Photocopy Body, Feet and Hand Patterns onto card stock—one set for each child. Cut yarn into 2-foot (60-cm) lengths—one for each child.

Instruct each child in the following procedures:
- Use crayons or felt pens to color face and clothes.
- Cut out Happy Healed Man's body, feet and hands.
- Cut short pieces of yarn and glue onto face to make hair and/or beard.
- Cut open four rubber bands.
- With teacher's help, staple a rubber band to each hand and foot (sketch a). Then staple opposite end of each rubber band to appropriate part of body.
- Use hole punch to punch hole in head.
- Cut a length of yarn, thread through hole and tie to make hanging loop (sketch b).

Bible Bits: Jesus performed many miracles and healed many people. One of the people Jesus healed was a man who couldn't walk. Why do you think Jesus healed people? Can you make your healed man jump with joy?

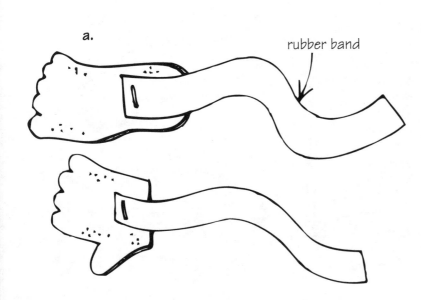

a.

rubber band

b.

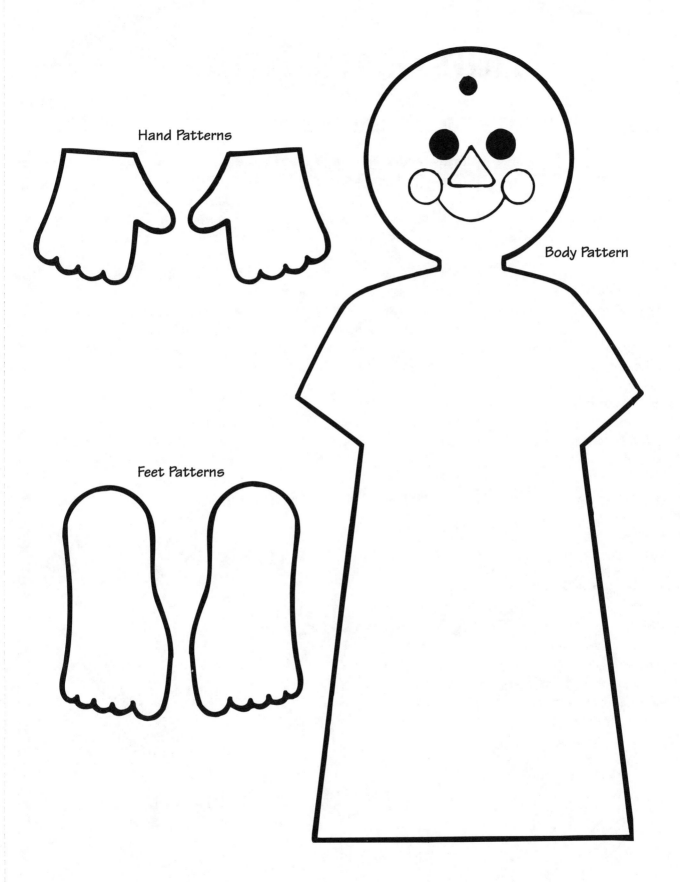

Hand Patterns

Body Pattern

Feet Patterns

LILIES OF THE FIELD
(25-30 MINUTES)

Materials
- Flower and Leaf Patterns
- small rocks or sand
- sphagnum moss (available at nurseries)
- salt

For each child—
- one small vegetable or soup can
- three green chenille wires
- two chenille wires in any color

Standard Supplies
- photocopier
- card stock in white, pink, yellow and green
- construction paper
- felt pens
- glue
- scissors
- ruler

Preparation: Photocopy Flower Patterns onto white, yellow and pink card stock—three flowers for each child. Photocopy Leaf Patterns onto green card stock—three leaves for each child. Cut construction paper into rectangles to fit around cans.

a.

Instruct each child in the following procedures:
- Cut out three flowers and three leaves.
- Apply glue to one side of flowers to make designs (sketch a).
- Sprinkle salt over glue. Shake off excess salt and set flowers aside to dry.
- Letter on construction paper rectangle "Consider how the lilies grow. Luke 12:27."
- Glue paper around can, making sure words are to the outside.
- Glue colored chenille wire around the top and bottom of soup can; trim if necessary.
- Glue a green chenille wire to center of each flower on the side with salt.

- Wrap the lower edges of flower together around stem to look like a calla lily and glue. Hold in place a few moments to dry (sketch b). Repeat for each flower.
- Fill can one-half full of rocks or sand.
- Insert flower stems and leaves into filled can.
- Place moss around flowers until it reaches the top of the can (sketch c).

Bible Bits: **You may use your flower arrangement as a paperweight or give it as a gift to remind people that God cares for us.**

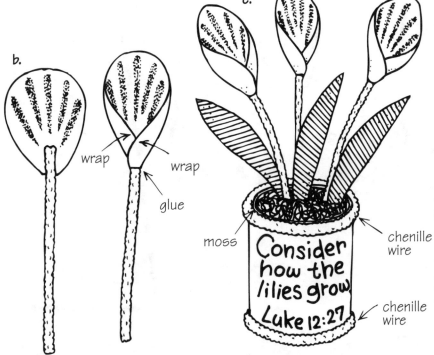

b.

wrap

wrap

glue

c.

moss

chenille wire

Consider how the lilies grow Luke 12:27

chenille wire

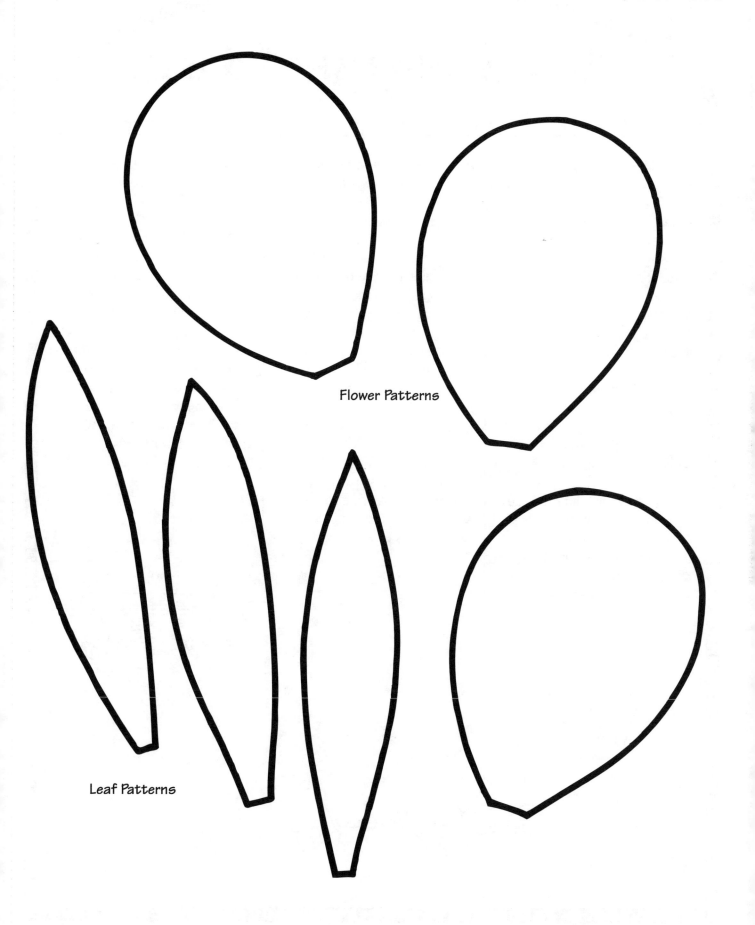

Flower Patterns

Leaf Patterns

"LOAVES AND FISHES" BASKET

(20-30 MINUTES)

Materials
- Basket Pattern
- raffia
- spring-type clothespins
- brightly colored poster board

Standard Supplies
- construction paper
- pencil
- felt pens
- glue
- scissors
- measuring stick

Preparation: Trace Basket Pattern onto poster board—one basket for each child. Cut out baskets. With point of scissors, score along dotted lines and bend flaps up to make sides of basket (sketch a). Cut raffia into 3-foot (90-cm) lengths—several for each child. Cut construction paper into 1×3-inch (2.5×7.5-cm) strips—five for each child.

Instruct each child in the following procedures:
- Letter "Jesus Cares for Me" in center of basket.
- Glue end of raffia length inside basket (sketch b). Weave raffia around the inside of one flap of basket and outside the next (sketch b). When one raffia length is completed, glue the end to the poster board and glue on a new raffia length. Continue weaving until raffia is ½ inch (1.25 cm) from top of basket. Cut raffia and fasten end with glue.
- Finish off top of basket by gluing on folded strips of construction paper (sketch c).
- Use clothespins to hold paper in place as glue dries (sketch c).

Simplification Idea: Use thick craft yarn or rug yarn instead of raffia.

Bible Bits: One time when Jesus was speaking to a large crowd of people, a little boy gave Jesus something to help feed all the people. What did the little boy give Jesus? (His lunch of five loaves and two fish.) Why do you think Jesus performed a miracle by multiplying the little boy's lunch? (Volunteers answer.) Jesus loves us and will always take care of our needs.

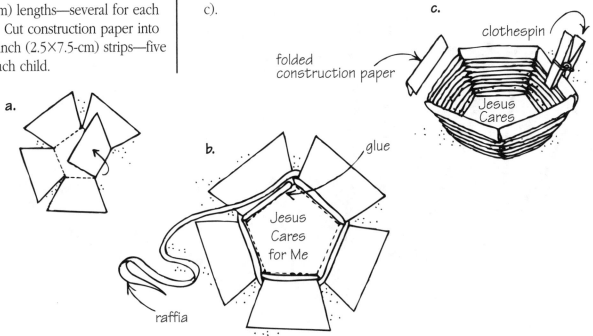

a.

b.

c.

folded construction paper

clothespin

Jesus Cares

Jesus Cares for Me

glue

raffia

BASKET PATTERN

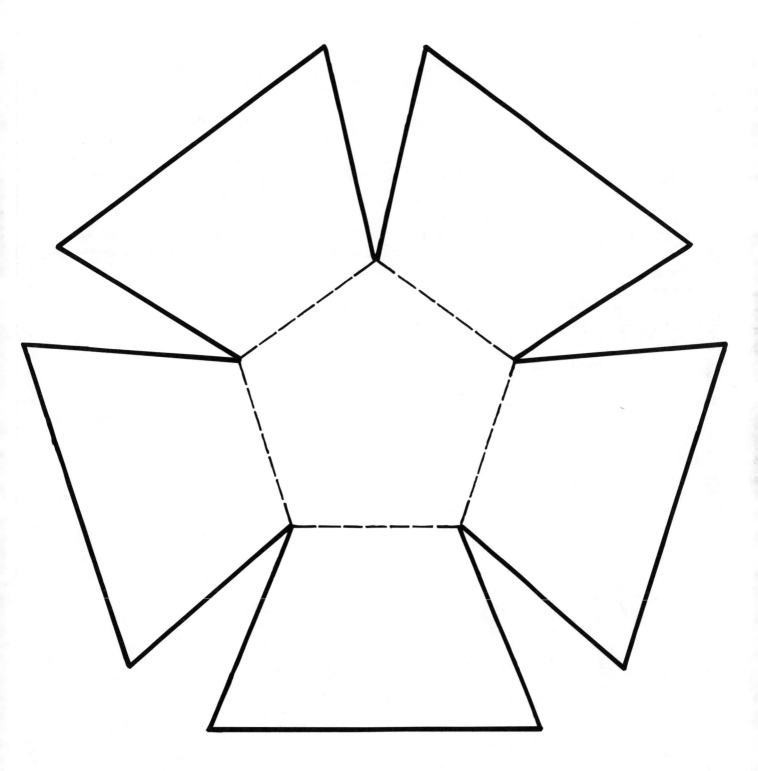

PAW-PRINT BOOKMARK
(20-30 MINUTES)

Materials
- Paw-Print Patterns
- felt
- yarn

Standard Supplies
- lightweight cardboard
- card stock
- pencils
- felt pens
- glue
- scissors
- ruler

Preparation: Trace Paw-Print Patterns onto cardboard to make one of each pattern for every two to three children. Cut yarn into 10-inch (25-cm) lengths—one for each child.

Instruct each child in the following procedures:
- Choose one pattern and trace onto card stock four times. Cut out.
- Cut shapes from felt for pads and claws, toenails or hooves and glue onto two of the prints (sketch a).
- With felt pen, letter "Lead us not" on third print and "into temptation" on fourth print (sketch b).
- Spread glue on backs of two lettered prints.
- Place one end of yarn on each glued print.
- Press two decorated prints onto the two glued prints, sealing in yarn.

Bible Bits: In the Bible, Jesus taught us to pray, "Lead us not into temptation," because He knows that God helps us stay away from trouble if we ask Him. Reading the Bible helps us know what to do when we are tempted to do wrong. You can use your Paw-Print Bookmark in your Bible. It will remind you that God leads you *away* from trouble, when you pray for His help.

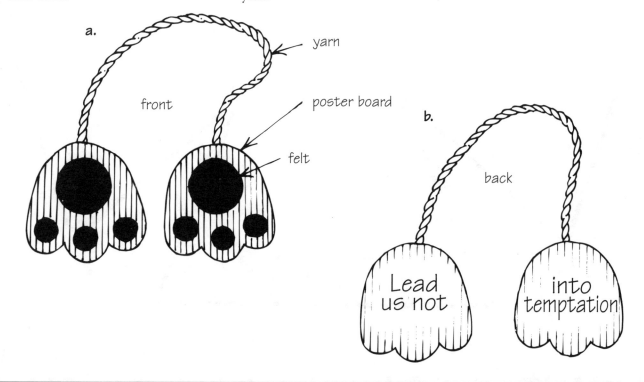

PAW-PRINT PATTERNS

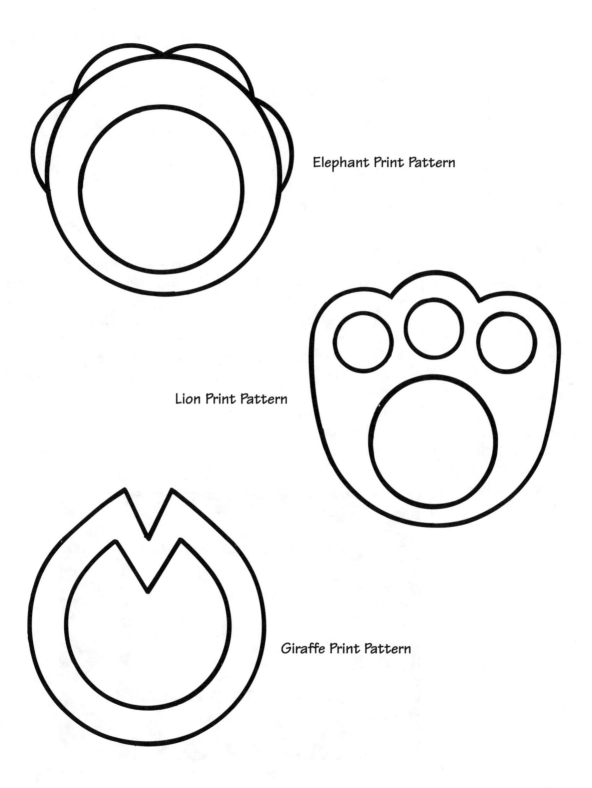

Elephant Print Pattern

Lion Print Pattern

Giraffe Print Pattern

"LORD'S PRAYER" PLACE MAT
(20-30 MINUTES)

Materials
◆ "Lord's Prayer" Pattern
◆ brown packaging paper or large paper grocery bags
◆ clear Con-Tact paper
◆ tempera paints
◆ objects to print with (such as vegetables or pieces of sponge)

Standard Supplies
◆ photocopier
◆ colored copier paper
◆ glue
◆ scissors
◆ measuring stick
◆ shallow containers
◆ newspaper
◆ measuring stick

Preparation: Cut packaging paper or grocery bags into 11×15-inch (27.5×37.5-cm) rectangles—one for each child. Cut Con-Tact paper into 12×16-inch (30×40-cm) rectangles—two for each child. Photocopy the "Lord's Prayer" Pattern onto colored paper—one for each child. Cover work area with newspaper. Pour paint into shallow containers.

Instruct each child in the following procedures:
◆ Crumple packaging paper or grocery bag rectangle into a small wad and then smooth out carefully. Repeat until paper is as soft as cloth.
◆ Cut out Lord's Prayer and glue onto paper rectangle (see sketch).
◆ Use paints and printing objects to decorate place mat. Let dry.
◆ Lay one piece of Con-Tact paper on table, sticky side up. Gently pull off backing.
◆ Place paper rectangle, prayer side down, on top of Con-Tact paper and smooth bubbles out from center. (Have children work in pairs on this step.)

◆ Partially pull off backing of second piece of Con-Tact paper. Lay sticky portion on back of place mat and continue peeling as you smooth it out.
◆ Trim edges of Con-Tact paper.

Enrichment Idea: Children letter prayer directly on place mat.

Bible Bits: **Who can say the Lord's Prayer from memory?** Allow those who know it to recite it together. **What is your favorite part of the prayer? Jesus taught His disciples how to pray, using this prayer as an example.**

Our Father which art in heaven, Hallowed be thy name. Thy kingdom come. Thy will be done in earth, as it is in heaven. Give us this day our daily bread. And forgive us our debts, as we forgive our debtors. And lead us not into temptation, but deliver us from evil: For thine is the kingdom, and the power, and the glory, for ever. Amen. Matthew 6:9-13 (KJV)

paper bag

clear Con-Tact paper

"LORD'S PRAYER" PATTERN

Our Father which art in heaven,
Hallowed be thy name. Thy kingdom come.
Thy will be done in earth, as it is in heaven.
Give us this day our daily bread.
And forgive us our debts, as we forgive our
debtors. And lead us not into temptation,
but deliver us from evil: For thine is
the kingdom, and the power, and the glory,
for ever. Amen.   Matthew 6:9-13 (KJV)

"LORD'S PRAYER" PLAQUE
(20-30 MINUTES)

Materials
- "Lord's Prayer" Pattern
- an assortment of decorating materials (braid, beads, feathers, shells, dried flowers and grasses, etc.)
- yarn

For each student—
- one basket-type paper-plate holder

Optional—
- hot-glue gun and glue sticks

Standard Supplies
- photocopier
- copier paper
- craft glue
- scissors
- ruler

Preparation: Photocopy "Lord's Prayer" Pattern onto paper—one for each student. Plug in glue gun out of reach of children.

Instruct each child in the following procedures:
- Cut out "Lord's Prayer" Pattern and glue onto plate holder.
- Decorate plate holder with braid, beads, feathers, etc. and glue in place. (*Optional:* With teacher's help, use glue gun to attach decorations to plate holder.)

- Cut a 4-inch (10-cm) length of braid or yarn. Form into a loop and glue onto back of basket for a hanger.

Bible Bits: **Who can say the Lord's Prayer?** Allow volunteers to say it. **Which is your favorite part of the prayer? Why?**

yarn

braid

dried flowers

Our Father
which art in heaven,
Hallowed be thy name.
Thy kingdom come.
Thy will be done in earth,
as it is in heaven.
Give us this day our daily bread.
And forgive us our debts,
as we forgive our debtors.
And lead us not into temptation,
but deliver us from evil:
For thine is the kingdom,
and the power, and the glory,
for ever. Amen.
Matthew 6:9-13 (KJV)

beads

feathers

"LORD'S PRAYER" PATTERN

Our Father
which art in heaven,
Hallowed be thy name.
Thy kingdom come.
Thy will be done in earth,
as it is in heaven.
Give us this day our daily bread.
And forgive us our debts,
as we forgive our debtors.
And lead us not into temptation,
but deliver us from evil:
For thine is the kingdom,
and the power, and the glory,
for ever. Amen.

Matthew 6:9-13 (KJV)

"DAILY BREAD" MAGNET
(25-30 MINUTES)

Materials
- Bread and Ribbon Patterns
- clear acrylic spray
- black yarn

For each child—
- one slice of mini-toast (found in cracker or deli sections of most grocery stores)
- two wiggle eyes
- one ½-inch (1.25-cm) round magnet

Standard Supplies
- photocopier
- card stock
- glue
- scissors
- ruler
- newspapers

Preparation: Photocopy Bread and Ribbon Patterns onto card stock—one set for each child. Cut yarn into 1-inch (2.5-cm) pieces—one for each child. On newspaper spray toast with clear acrylic spray.

Instruct each child in the following procedures:
- Glue wiggle eyes to toast.
- Glue yarn on toast to make smile.
- Cut out Bread Pattern.
- Glue toast to bread cutout (sketch a).
- Cut out Ribbon Patterns.
- Glue magnet to back of bread cutout. (Make sure glue is applied to repellent side, not magnetic side.)
- Glue ribbons to back of bread cutout (sketch b).

Bible Bits: **The Bible says God will give us the things we need to grow. We can pray to God and say, "Give us this day our daily bread." What are some other things that God has given to you?** (Family, friends, pets, etc.) **Your "Daily Bread" Magnet can remind you to thank God for the people who care for you and the things He has given you.**

Ribbon Patterns

Give us this day our

daily bread.

Bread Pattern

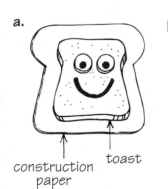

a.

construction paper   toast

b.

Give us this day our daily bread.

MASTER'S MONEY BAG
(15-20 MINUTES)

Materials
- muslin fabric
- a variety of coins
- 1-mm leatherlike cording
- an awl or hole punch

Optional—
- chocolate or play coins

Standard Supplies
- crayons in a variety of colors
- fabric scissors
- transparent tape
- measuring stick
- pencil

Preparation: Cut muslin into 9-inch (22.5-cm) circles—one for each child. Cut cording into 24-inch (60-cm) lengths—one for each child. Wrap tape around one end of each cord. Use awl or hole punch to make 20 evenly spaced holes about 1 inch (2.5 cm) from edge of circle (sketch a). Make sure holes are large enough for children to thread cording through.

Instruct each child in the following procedures:
- Choose a coin and crayon. Wrap muslin cloth tightly around coin and rub crayon across top of covered coin to make an imprint (sketch b).
- Continue crayon rubbing process all over muslin circle, using different-sized coins and different-colored crayons.
- Tie a knot in untaped end of cord.
- Beginning on the colored side of fabric, weave taped end of cord in and out of holes (sketch c).
- Pull ends of cording together to gather muslin to form a pouch (sketch d).
- Wrap and tie ends together.
- *Optional:* Place chocolate or play coins in pouch.

Bible Bits: **Jesus told a story about a master who was going on a trip. He called his three servants and gave them his money to take care of while he was gone. Two of the servants were helpful. They used the money to make even *more* money for their master. The other servant was lazy. What do you think he did with the money?** (Children respond.) **He buried it in the ground and didn't do *anything*. When the master came back, whom do you think he rewarded? Whom do you think got fired?** (Children respond.) **Jesus told this story to teach us that He wants us to use the abilities and talents He has given to us to do good things. So don't hide your talents! (Terence), what is something you like to do with your talents?**

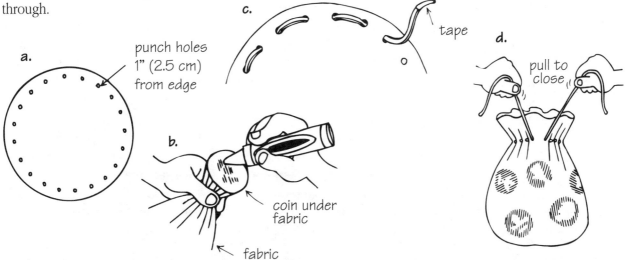

a.

punch holes 1" (2.5 cm) from edge

b.

coin under fabric

fabric

c.

tape

d.

pull to close

The Big Book of Bible Crafts

"PRODIGAL SON" FINGER PUPPETS

(20 MINUTES FOR EACH PUPPET)

Materials

- Finger Puppet Patterns
- pink and brown yarn
- felt pieces in various colors including peach, pink, yellow, brown and gray
- 4-mm wiggle eyes
- heart-shaped plastic confetti
- straight pins
- sewing machine and thread
- black fine-tip permanent felt pens

Standard Supplies

- photocopier
- card stock
- pen
- glue
- scissors

Preparation: For each puppet: With pen, trace Puppet Body Pattern onto felt (pink felt for Pig puppet; any other colors of felt for Father, Older Brother and Runaway Son). Pin a second layer of same-colored felt to the traced felt pieces. Machine stitch through both layers of felt on traced lines, leaving the bottom edge of each puppet open (sketch a). Cut around the stitching line of each finger puppet, leaving about a ⅛-inch (.3125-cm) seam. Do not turn right side out. The stitching line should show.

Photocopy remaining Puppet Patterns onto several sheets of card stock. Cut out.

For Pig Puppet:

- Trace Pig Head, Nose and Foot Patterns onto pink felt. Trace Corn Pattern onto yellow felt. Cut out.
- Glue head, nose, corn and feet to front of pink felt puppet body (sketch b).
- Cut a small piece of pink yarn and glue to the back of Pig Puppet for a tail.
- With felt pen, draw nostrils and mouth.
- Glue on two wiggle eyes.

For Father, Older-Brother and Runaway-Son Puppets:

- Trace Face Pattern and Hand Patterns onto peach felt. Cut out.
- Trace Sleeve Patterns onto felt colors to match the puppet body. Cut out.
- Trace Beard Pattern onto felt and cut out—use gray felt for Father's beard and brown felt for Runaway Son's and Older Brother's beards.
- Trace Head Wrap onto felt. Cut out.
- Glue face near the top of puppet body.
- Glue sleeves to the back of puppet (sketch c).
- Glue brown yarn belt to the front of Older-Brother Puppet.
- Glue the two Hand A felt pieces to the front of Father and Older-Brother Puppets and

Hand B to the front of Runaway-Son Puppet. Wrap the sleeves to the front. Glue in place (sketch c).

- Glue beard on face.
- Glue the short end of Head Wrap to the front of puppet head.
- Fold the Head Wrap over top of puppet and glue to back side (sketch d). Press Head Wrap down until glue holds it in place.
- Glue two wiggle eyes on puppet. Glue heart-shaped confetti on Father Puppet.
- Using the permanent pen, add facial features to puppet (sketch e).

Bible Bits: **Jesus told the story of "The Prodigal Son," a boy who left home and spent all his money foolishly. When the son decided to return home, he was sorry for what he had done. What was he willing to do?** (Work for his father as a servant.) **How did the son's father react?** (He forgave him and had a big party to celebrate the return of his son.) **What did the older brother do?** (He was angry that his father forgave his brother.) **Jesus told this story to show us that God loves us like the father loved the prodigal son. He will always forgive us if we are sorry for the wrong things we do.**

a.

b.

wiggle eyes   head

nose

corn
feet

c.

glue to back

back   front

glue head wrap
to front

wrap and
glue to back

d.

e.

heart
confetti

yarn
belt

Father   Runaway Son   Older Brother

Finger Puppet Patterns

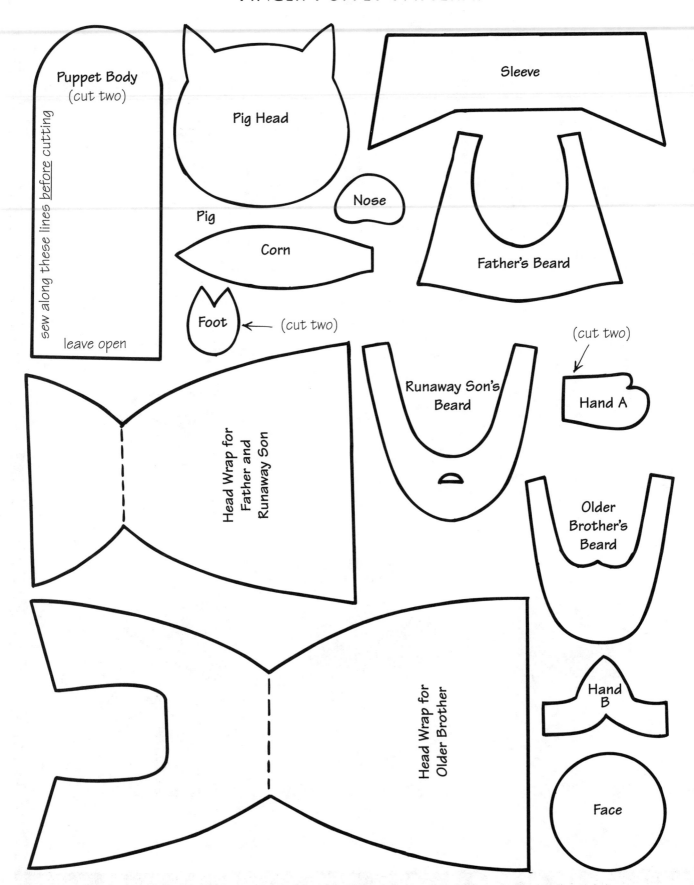

Puppet Body
(cut two)

sew along these lines before cutting

leave open

Pig Head

Pig

Corn

Foot   ← (cut two)

Sleeve

Nose

Father's Beard

Head Wrap for Father and Runaway Son

Runaway Son's Beard

(cut two)

Hand A

Older Brother's Beard

Head Wrap for Older Brother

Hand B

Face

FEED THE PIG
(20 MINUTES)

Materials
- Pig Face Patterns
- pink chenille wire
- white and pink Fun Foam or construction paper
- pink tissue paper

For each child—
- one small, clear plastic take-out box

Standard Supplies
- lightweight cardboard
- black felt pens
- craft glue
- scissors

Preparation: Trace several copies of Pig Face Patterns onto lightweight cardboard, label and cut out. Cut chenille wires in half—one half for each child.

Instruct each child in the following procedures:
- Using ear and nose cardboard patterns, trace two ears and one nose onto pink Fun Foam. Cut out.
- Trace two eyes onto white Fun Foam using eye cardboard pattern. Cut out.
- Squeeze glue on the straight edge of each ear piece. Pinch the sides together and hold until dry (sketch a).
- Use black felt pen to make dots on the eyes and nose (sketch b).
- Lightly crumple up tissue paper

and place inside box. Close lid.
- Glue ears, nose and eyes onto the top portion of box at the front opening.
- Wrap chenille wire around your finger to curl pig's tail. Glue the tail to the hinged side of box (sketch b).
- You can "feed" your pig with whatever you want to collect inside the box, or you can put candy or a gift inside and give it to someone you love!

Bible Bits: In the Bible, Jesus tells a story about a son who left home. He spent all his money on parties. Soon he had nothing left and had to get a job feeding pigs. The son was miserable. He knew he had done wrong but decided to go home anyway. Was his father angry when he saw his son? (No. He forgave him.) **God loves us like this father loved his son. Even when we do things we know are wrong, God still loves and forgives us.**

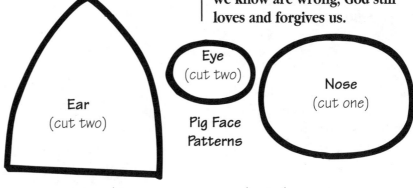

Ear
(cut two)

Eye
(cut two)

Nose
(cut one)

Pig Face
Patterns

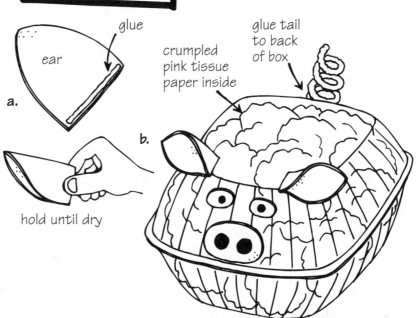

a.
glue
ear
hold until dry

b.
crumpled
pink tissue
paper inside

glue tail
to back
of box

ANGEL BOOKMARK
(15-20 MINUTES)

Materials
- Angel Bookmark Pattern
- 3/4-inch (1.9-cm) ribbon in various colors
- poster board

Standard Supplies
- pencil
- felt pens
- glue
- scissors
- stapler and staples
- ruler

Preparation: Trace Angel Bookmark Pattern onto poster board and cut out—one for each child. Cut ribbon for streamers into 6-inch (15-cm) lengths—four for each child. Cut ribbon for waistbands into 3-inch (7.5-cm) lengths—one for each child.

Instruct each child in the following procedures:
- Use felt pens to draw the angel's facial features and hair.
- Staple ribbon streamers to the waist of the angel (sketch a).
- Glue ribbon waistband over staples to hide staples and raw edges (sketch b).
- Glue ends of waistband to back of bookmark (sketch c).
- To use as a bookmark, place arms of angel across page you want to mark (sketch d).

Bible Bits: **What did the angel in our Bible story do? Can you find the story in your Bible and mark it with your Angel Bookmark?**

a. poster board / staple / ribbon
b.
c.
d.

ANGEL BOOKMARK PATTERN

CLOTHESPIN CROSS
(20-25 MINUTES)

Materials
- metallic gold thread
- 1½-inch (3.75-cm) ribbon

For each child—
- five spring-type clothespins

Standard Supplies
- craft glue
- scissors
- measuring stick

Preparation: Remove springs from clothespins. Cut ribbon into 15-inch (37.5-cm) and 9-inch (22.5-cm) lengths—one of each for each student. Cut metallic thread into 4-inch (10-cm) lengths—one for each student.

Instruct each child in the following procedures:
- Fold 1 inch (2.5 cm) of longer piece of ribbon to the back and crease it.
- Tie and knot ends of metallic thread together.
- Place tied metallic thread inside the fold of ribbon and glue folded portion together to form hanger (sketch a).
- Fold shorter piece of ribbon in half to find midpoint.
- Glue midpoint of shorter ribbon across longer ribbon about 5 inches (12.5 cm) from top, forming a cross (sketch b).

- Glue four clothespin pieces (two pieces wide and flat side down) onto horizontal bar of ribbon. Repeat procedure on vertical bar of ribbon, using six clothespin pieces (sketch c).

Bible Bits: **Why do you think Jesus died on the cross?** (Children respond.) **Why do you think He rose again from the dead?** (Children respond.) **Jesus' death and resurrection were part of God's loving plan to forgive our sins and give us eternal life.**

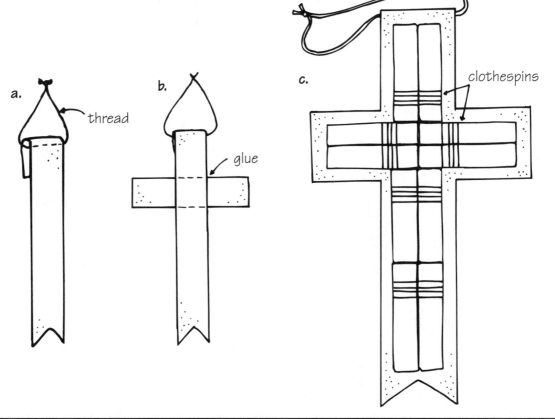

a. thread

b. glue

c. clothespins

EASTER CROSS
(25-30 MINUTES)

Materials
- 1-inch (2.5-cm) wooden doll pin stand
- felt
- jumbo craft sticks
- regular craft sticks
- purple fabric
- thread

For each child—
- one bunch artificial flowers on a wire stem

Standard Supplies
- hot-glue gun and glue sticks
- heavy-duty scissors
- ruler

Preparation: Use a doll pin stand as a pattern and trace circles onto felt—one circle for each child. Cut out circles. Cut purple fabric into 1½×7-inch (3.75×17.5-cm) and 3×8-inch (7.5×20-cm) strips. Use scissors to cut a blunt point in one end of jumbo craft stick (sketch a). Plug in glue gun out of reach of children.

Instruct each child in the following procedures:
- For swag, use fingers to gather one end of 3×8-inch (7.5×20-cm) fabric strip. Tie and knot thread around gathers. Cut thread ends. Repeat on other end of fabric. Glue gathered ends of fabric on opposite ends of one regular craft stick (sketch b).
- Glue felt circle to bottom of doll pin stand.
- With teacher's help, fill doll pin stand hole with hot glue. When glue is partially set, stick cut end of jumbo stick in glue and hold in place until glue sets. (For added strength, add a little more glue where stick and stand meet.)
- To make crossbeam, glue craft stick with swag horizontally on front of jumbo stick, 3/4 inches (1.9 cm) from top (sketch c).
- Glue second regular craft stick behind crossbeam to the back of jumbo stick and gathered ends of fabric swag (sketch d).
- To finish banner, fold long edges of remaining fabric strip to the center to hide raw edges. Fold strip in half over one end of swag and crossbeam (sketch e). Glue in place. Wrap stemmed flowers around bottom of cross.

Bible Bits: **We know that Jesus rose from the dead because He appeared to many people. To whom did He appear?** (Children respond.) **Some of His disciples, like John, Luke, Mark and Matthew wrote what they saw and heard from Jesus after He was resurrected. Today we can read their accounts in the Bible and learn the truth about Jesus ourselves.**

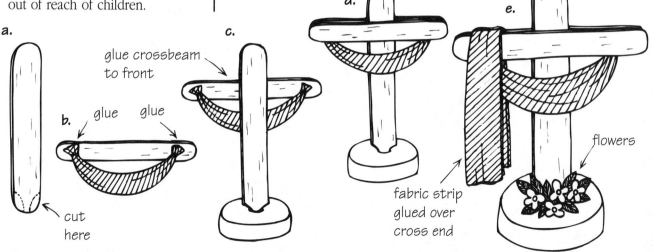

a.

b.   glue   glue

cut here

glue crossbeam to front

c.

d.

e.

fabric strip glued over cross end

flowers

"I LOVE JESUS" BOOKMARK

(15-20 MINUTES)

Materials
- yarn
- poster board

For each child—
- two 1-inch (2.5-cm) sticker pictures of Jesus (available at Christian supply stores)

Standard Supplies
- felt pens
- scissors
- hole punch
- ruler

Preparation: Cut yarn into 6-inch (15-cm) lengths—one for each child. Cut poster board into ½×4½-inch (3.75×11.25-cm) strips—one for each child. Punch a hole near the top of each piece.

Instruct each child in the following procedures:
- With a felt pen, letter the word "I" near top of poster-board strip.
- Draw a heart shape beneath "I." Color the heart.
- Attach sticker picture of Jesus beneath heart.
- Letter "because..." at the bottom of bookmark (sketch a).
- Turn over bookmark. Attach sticker picture near the top.
- Letter the word "first" beneath picture.
- Draw a heart beneath "first" and color in shape.
- Letter the word "ME" beneath heart (sketch b).
- Fold yarn in half. Push yarn fold through punched hole. Then insert yarn ends through yarn loop and pull to secure yarn to bookmark hole.

Bible Bits: **Listen to this Bible verse and then tell why we love Jesus.** Read 1 John 4:19. ***We love because he first loved us.*** **Jesus loves us. And He makes it possible for us to do something very special and important. Listen to find out what it is.** Read 1 John 4:7. ***Let us love one another, for love comes from God.*** **We can love one another because love comes from God.**

a.

b.

ROCK MOSAIC
(10-15 MINUTES)

Materials
- premixed tile-grout adhesive (available at home-improvement stores)
- aquarium rocks in various colors
- large spoons

For each child—
- one wide-mouth canning-jar ring and lid

Standard Supplies
- shallow containers

Preparation: Pour each color of rocks into separate shallow containers. Place canning-jar lids in rings.

Instruct each child in the following procedures:
- Use spoon to fill lids with grout, leaving about a ⅛-inch (.3125-cm) space at the top.
- Push colored aquarium rocks into the grout to make a cross or fish design (see sketch).
- Use one or two contrasting colors of rocks to fill in the rest of lid.
- Allow to dry overnight. The grout will take several days to harden completely.
- When dry, you may give your mosaic to someone to use as a coaster or trivet.

Bible Bits: Long ago in the Middle Ages, people built great churches called cathedrals. Artists made pictures called mosaics by using small pieces of rock and tile. Often they made *huge* pictures on the walls or floors of a church. The pictures showed stories from the Bible. Often they used Christian symbols as decoration. **What does the cross symbol stand for?** (Jesus died for our sins.) **What does the fish symbol mean?** (It was a sign used by early Christians to identify themselves as followers of Christ.)

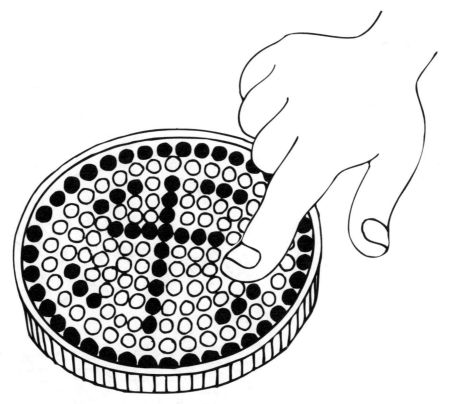

PRAYER JOURNAL
(20-25 MINUTES)

Materials
- tissue paper in various colors
- craft knife
- white poster board

For each child—
- two paper fasteners

Standard Supplies
- sheets of white paper
- glue
- paintbrushes
- scissors
- hole punch
- measuring stick
- shallow containers
- water
- newspaper

Preparation: Cut some of the poster board into 9×13-inch (22.5×32.5-cm) rectangles—one for each child. Use craft knife to score two lines ½ inch (1.25-cm) apart on each piece of poster board as shown in sketch a. Use a hole punch to punch two holes in poster board 3 inches (7.5 cm) from outside edges and ½ inch (1.25 cm) below second scored line (sketch a). Punch two holes at the top of sheets of paper (the same distance apart as holes in poster board). Cut remaining poster board into 9×12-inch (22.5×30-cm) rectangles—one for each child. Cover work area with newspaper. Dilute glue with a small amount of water in containers.

Instruct each child in the following procedures:
- Tear tissue paper into different size pieces.
- Brush glue mixture onto smaller poster-board piece.
- Place torn tissue paper onto sticky surface, one piece at a time, to create a design or picture (sketch b).
- Brush more glue over torn tissue paper. Allow to dry.
- Fold larger poster-board piece along score lines.
- Glue top edge of small poster board onto front flap of larger poster board (sketch c).
- Insert paper fasteners into holes to secure paper inside journal (sketch d).

Bible Bits: **In your Prayer Journal you can write your prayers and the names of people you want to pray for, or you can draw a picture of something you want to pray about. God wants us to spend time with Him in prayer. He listens to us when we pray out loud. He hears the prayers we think silently. He even knows the prayers we write to Him. God always listens!**

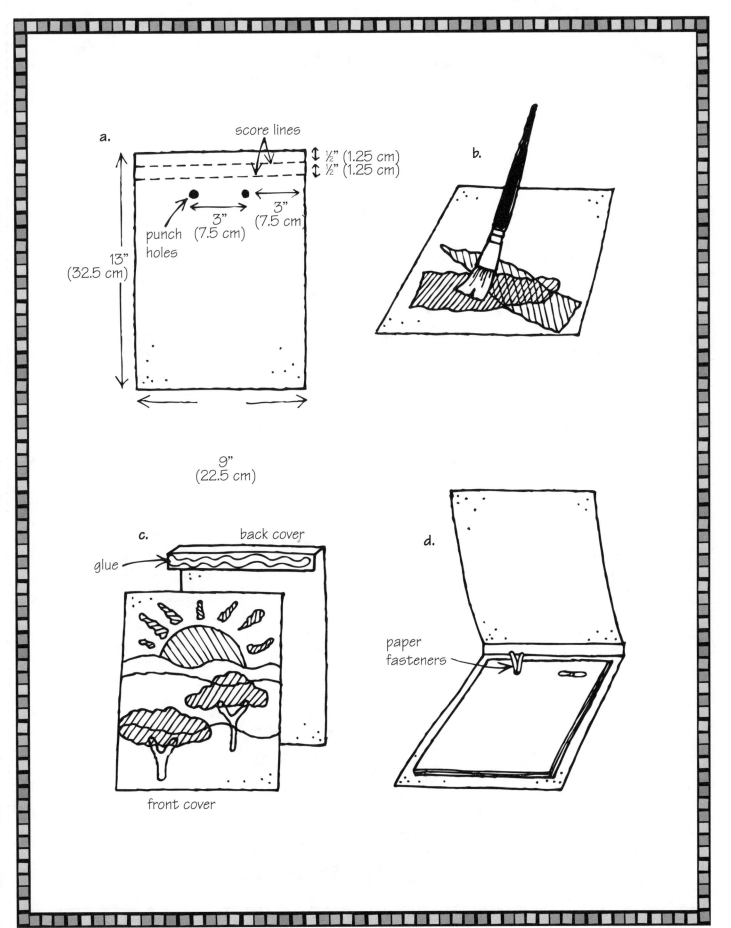

a.

score lines

½" (1.25 cm)
½" (1.25 cm)

punch holes

3" (7.5 cm)

3" (7.5 cm)

13" (32.5 cm)

9" (22.5 cm)

b.

c.

back cover

glue

front cover

d.

paper fasteners

"GOD'S WORD" COLLECTION

(25-30 MINUTES)

Materials
- Bibles
- several classified sections of newspaper
- index cards
- rickrack or other trim

For each child—
- one empty cake-mix box (or box of similar size)
- one jumbo craft stick

Standard Supplies
- chalkboard and chalk or butcher paper and felt pen
- colored card stock
- felt pens
- glue
- scissors
- ruler

Preparation: Cut each box to stand 5 inches (12.5 cm) tall. Discard the tops of boxes. On chalkboard or butcher paper letter the words "Wisdom, knowledge and understanding come from God's Word." Cut card stock in half—one half for each child.

Instruct each child in the following procedures:
- Glue paper from the classified section of the newspaper onto outside of box to cover completely.
- Cut the word "classified" from the headline of page and glue to covered box; then letter "Bible Verses" on box (sketch a).
- Glue rickrack or other trim around box.
- With felt pen, write the words written on the chalkboard onto card-stock piece.
- Glue one end of craft stick to the back of card stock to make a sign. Glue the other end of stick to the back of box (sketch b). Lay flat to dry.

- On an index card, letter Proverbs 9:10 from the Bible (sketch c). Place card in box.
- *Optional:* Letter John 8:12 and 14:15 (or other verses of your choice) on the other index cards.

Bible Bits: **You can keep your cards in your "classified" box and see how many verses you can memorize. What have you learned about God's Word? Why is it important to learn God's Word?**

c.

Proverbs 9:10

The fear of the Lord is the beginning of wisdom, and knowledge of the Holy One is understanding.

b.

Wisdom, knowledge and understanding come from God's Word

a.

SEED-PACKET BOOKMARK

(20-30 MINUTES)

Materials
- Bibles
- narrow ribbons in five various colors

For each child—
- one empty seed packet
- five unlined index cards

Standard Supplies
- felt pens
- crayons or colored pencils
- glue
- scissors
- measuring stick

Preparation: Cut index cards to fit inside seed packets. Cut ribbon into 15-inch (37.5-cm) lengths—five different colors for each child.

Instruct each child in the following procedures:
- Letter names and draw pictures of the first five fruit of the Spirit: Love, Joy, Peace, Patience and Kindness—one on each index card (sketch a).
- Tie ends of ribbons together leaving 1 inch (2.5 cm) below knot (sketch b).
- Glue ribbons onto back of seed packet, 2 inches (5 cm) above knot (sketch c). Let dry.
- Place index cards inside seed packet.
- Place bookmark inside Bible to mark Galatians 5:22,23. Use ribbons to mark a verse for each fruit of the Spirit. (Love—John 15:12; Joy—Psalms 126:3; Peace—John 14:27; Patience—Ephesians 4:2; Kindness—1 Thessalonians 5:15.)

Enrichment Idea: Children design index cards for additional four fruit of the Spirit. Mark verses. (Goodness—Matthew 5:16; Faithfulness—Proverbs 3:3; Gentleness—Proverbs 15:1; Self-control—Philippians 4:13.)

Bible Bits: What are the first five fruit of the Spirit? (Love, joy, peace, patience, kindness.) **Do you think you will be able to remember these next week? next year? Use your Seed-Packet Bookmark to help you. Every time you open your Bible, try to recite the fruit of the Spirit. Then look inside your seed packet to check. Learning the names of the fruit of the Spirit will help us remember to show these qualities at home, school, church or wherever we go!**

a.
kindness
Patience
Peace
Joy
Love

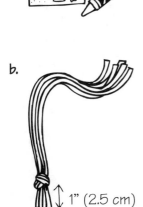

b.

1" (2.5 cm)

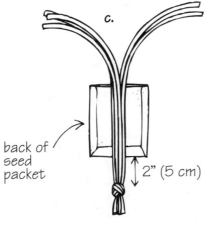

c.

back of seed packet

2" (5 cm)

Galatians

Wildflower Seeds

The Big Book of Bible Crafts

"NEW CREATION" BUTTERFLY
(15-20 MINUTES)

Materials
- black fine-tip permanent felt pens
- tissue paper in a variety of bright colors
- chenille wire

For each child—
- one large round-head wooden clothespin (nonspring-type)

Standard Supplies
- scissors
- ruler

Preparation: Cut tissue paper into pieces the following sizes: 4×6 inches (10×15 cm), 5×6 inches (12.5×15 cm), 6×6 inches (15×15 cm), 6×7 inches (15×17.5 cm)—one of each for each child. If possible, provide a variety of colors, so children may choose color combinations and each child's butterfly will be unique.

Instruct each child in the following procedures:
- Use felt pen to draw eyes and mouth on head of clothespin.
- Select four different-sized sheets of tissue paper to use for the butterfly wings.
- Lay tissue sheets one on top of the other, largest on bottom and smallest on top (sketch a).
- Slide tissue sheets into opening of clothespin. Gather tissue so it is about 1 inch (2.5 cm) from bottom of clothespin (sketch b).
- Bend chenille wire in half. Place midpoint at "neck" and twist in back, extending ends evenly upward. Curl ends of wire to make antennae.

Bible Bits: Who can tell me what is special about a butterfly? Lead children to tell the process a caterpillar goes through to become a butterfly. **The Bible says that when we believe in Jesus, we change into something new, too! We don't look different, but we *are* different inside because God's Spirit comes into our lives and helps us become more like Him.**

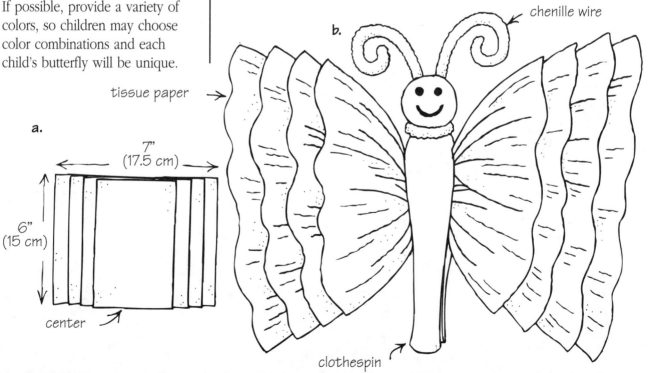

chenille wire

b.

tissue paper →

a.

7" (17.5 cm)

6" (15 cm)

center →

clothespin →

INDEX